The Vanishing Indigenous Heritage of the Abagusii of Western Kenya

John S. Akama, Herman O. Kiriama & Joshua N. Araka

Nsemia

First Edition: August 2024

Published by: Nsemia Inc. Publishers (www.nsemia.com)
Oakville, Ontario, Canada

Edited by: Nsemia Inc. Publishers
Cover Concept by: Authors
Cover Illustration by: Robert Kambo
Cover Design by: Linda Kiboma
Layout Design: Bethsheba Nyabuto
Photography: Courtesy of Joshua N. Araka

Note for Librarians:

A cataloguing record for this book is available from Kenya National Library Services.

ISBN: 978-9914-760-13-2

Acknowledgements

We acknowledge the extraordinary support and encouragement we received from individuals and groups that we interacted with while we undertook field research that formed the basis of this book project.

While it may not be possible to mention all of them, we single out Zebedee Obara, Tabitha Obonyo, Joseph Otenyo and Teresa Kiage of the Tabaka area. The four were instrumental in sharing with us many perspectives of soapstone and granite as key and strategic resources that exist within the borders of Kisii.

David Apoko of the Ogembo area in Kisii County, Joseck Ongeri and Morara Kirera of Manga, Nyamira County, gave us insights and leads to several aspects that have been documented in this book. We substantially benefited from the extensive knowledge of Pastor (retired) Nahashon Moronya, of the Seventh-Day Adventist Church, which he generously shared with us.

We appreciate the support we received from all others (many of them) who helped us in one way or the other. You encouraged us, pointed us to sources we might not have and influenced our perspectives as we put together this work. We thank them unreservedly.

List of Acronyms

BCE	Before the Common Era
BNP	Button Necked Pottery
DCs	District Commissioners
DOs	Divisional Officers
ICOMOS	International Council on Monuments and Sites
KSW	Kisii Soft Ware
PCs	Provincial Commissioners
SDA	Seventh-Day Adventist
UN	United Nations
UNESCO	United Nations Educational, Scientific and Cultural Organization

Table of Contents

Preface

Heritage is an important aspect of any community; it gives a community an identity and sense of belonging. This heritage is operationalised through places (tangibles) and elements (intangibles). The past elders of the community appreciated the role of these places and therefore took every effort to ensure their preservation.

Since the 1970s when the United Nations started talking of sustainable development of communities, heritage has come to be recognised as one of the resources that can be used in improving the livelihoods of communities. But despite this recognition, heritage especially in African countries, is under siege from various corners including armed conflict, terrorism, climate change, illicit trafficking, neglect, natural disasters, population growth, and the cultural erosion because of development pressures such as construction of roads, energy, and housing. Heritage places are being destroyed to give way to "development."

Despite this nationalisation or internationalisation of heritage and its usage as an economic resource, however, heritage is local, it has its foundations on the belief systems, ways of life of particular local communities. These communities use heritage in its various configurations, both tangible and intangible, to identify themselves; to construct who they are as a people and a community. There is need therefore for communities to preserve and protect their heritage places. Not only as places that give these communities identity, but also as an economic resource that can enable communities uplift their livelihoods.

This book is therefore a response to the need of understanding and unmasking Abagusii heritage places to both the local and international communities. It is meant to make the Abagusii people know, understand, and appreciate their heritage places and the intangible elements associated with them. This is urgent especially in the face of the generational change that is happening, as many older people who have the knowledge of these heritage places pass away. Further, as many Abagusii people move out of the homeland to other parts of the country and even abroad, and as those who remain home are increasingly adopting "modern" culture, there is present fear that unless urgent steps are taken to preserve them, most of these places and their associated intangible elements will disappear.

By documenting these heritage places, and their foundations, it is hoped that the two county governments of Gusiiland, Kisii and Nyamira, will take steps to protect these places, by establishing a register of all important heritage places in their jurisdictions and setting aside budgetary allocation for their conservation. It is also hoped that the two county governments and community organisations will use these heritage places not only as tourism resources, but also as communal identity markers. Furthermore, it is hoped that the book will raise awareness among the community members to extent that they will take steps to protect heritage places within their vicinity.

Chapter One

Cultural Heritage

Introduction

This book aims to study the heritage sites of Gusiiland, to understand their location, their history, the belief systems associated with them and their importance to the Abagusii people. Before doing that, however, we first look at what is heritage the type of heritage that exists and how the modern heritage preservation movement started. This will enable us to situate the Gusiiland heritage sites and anchor any argument that may be put forward for the preservation of these sites.

The Abagusii

Abagusii are a group of the Bantu-speaking people of Eastern Africa. The Bantu are said to have occupied this part of Africa, coming by way of the Congo Forest around the 3rd century before the Common Era (BCE). The contention is that the Bantu might have originated in the Nigeria-Cameroon border. From here, they dispersed east-westwards to occupy Eastern and Western parts of Africa and then spread north-southwards to occupy the northern and southern parts of the African continent. It is in this nucleus dispersal area that the Bantu are said to have acquired their Bantu characteristics. The Bantus were mostly farmers but are also said to have acquired the art of cattle keeping from the southern Cushites whom they encountered as they spread from their nucleus home.

According to Abagusii oral traditions, the Abagusii and other related people such as the Abaluyia, Agikuyu and Ameru, originated in a place known as *Misri*. This area should not be confused with the biblical Egypt but according to some historians such as Ochieng' (1971), this area could be somewhere in northern Uganda/Southern Sudan. The Abagusii are said to have occupied their present homeland at around 1500 CE.

Alternatively, this Misri narrative might have been borrowed from the Bible imitating the idea of the migration of the Israelites from Egypt to the Promised Land. From Misri the Abagusii are said to have moved southwards and sojourned for a while in the Mt. Elgon area of western Kenya and Eastern Uganda. According to Abagusii's oral history, Nyakomogendi, Mogusii's mother, took her sons from the Mt. Elgon area to Lake Victoria which received more rain and had fertile soils good for cultivation. They followed River Nzoia (then called Manyanza) until they reached Lake Victoria. At first, they sojourned/at Ramogi hills, and afterwards, they moved to Kisumu which, however, they found not to be conducive for cultivation. They therefore left the place, with the Moragoli going northwards and Mogusii and Mogikoyo (ancestor of the Agikuyu) going eastwards. Nyakomogendi is said to have been so old that she decided not to move from Kisumu, but she told her children to go and look for good land suitable for cultivation. To prevent their mother from dying of hunger, the children are said to have cooked for her ten baskets (*ebiee*) of ugali and left them for her.

Mogusii and Mogikoyo went eastwards until they reached Sondu where they are said to have parted, with Mogikoyo going northeastwards through the Rift Valley up to his present settlement. Mogusii went southwards up to Masosa (or Ngoina Hill) in north Mogirango. This might mean that either Mogusii did not sojourn in Kano or his sojourn there was very short.

However, there is evidence of Abagusii passing through Kano or a swamp place since it is said that wherever Mogusii passed, he named one of his daughters after that place. Thus following this theory, it can be stated that Mogusii did not pass through Lake Victoria but may have passed through the edges of the lake (*ekemunto*) and named one of his daughters Kemunto. He must have also passed through a swampy place because he named one of his daughters Kerubo (Ekerubo — swampy place). This might mean that the Abagusii had a very brief stop at the Kano plains, more probably at Sondu where they are said to have parted with Mogikoyo. Evidence to support the sojourney at Sondu is that after traversing through a swampy place, the Abagusii, it is said, came to a place where they crossed a river and named their daughter Kwamboka (crossing).

Immediately after crossing, it is said they descended a hill which was full of a certain ritualistic tree called *omoraa*, and they named their daughter Moraa. Now, immediately after leaving Sondu, coming by way of Nyamira, at Masosa, there is a hill which is full of this tree called *omoraa*. So, we infer that after Sondu, the Abagusii settled at Masosa (sometimes referred to by other people as Ng'oina Hill).

From Masosa, Abagusii went to Wire Hills in South Nyanza, which, however, they did not like. They then left and went again back to Masosa. From Masosa, they went to Kabianga in Kericho where they cultivated grains and kept livestock. But the grains never did well despite all the efforts, and cattle died. This might have been due to the cold. They thus said "Kabianga, Togende" (since they have refused, let us go). They then crossed River Sondu and sojourned at Riasiango which today is called Shiongori in Chepalungu. The patriarch Mogusii is said to have died here.

The remaining descendants of Mogusii again crossed river Mogori and went to the Mara area in today's Maasai and Kurialand. Other Abagusii — children of Mogirango — refused to leave Shiongori. They instead went westwards and stayed in today's north and west Mogirango. These are today's Abanyamatuta, Abagichora, Abakimori and Abaisanga.

Those who went to Mara, moved further southwest to Karungu in South Nyanza. These were the children of Ibabe, who was the son of Mosweta. It is said that two of Mosweta's sons moved south to Basutoland (Lesotho - this however, has not been ascertained. There is a need to explore whether there is a clan known by such a name in Lesotho). Another one remained in South Nyanza to give rise to the Kuria and others went northwards up to *Inani* (forest) in Wanjare. These were Omachoge, Nyaribari, Ogetutu, Mobasi, Osamaro, Omorangi, Osigisa and Mosoba who were the last born.

From the above narration, we can conclude, that the Abagusii adopted their present name quite recently — sometime after leaving the cradle land. This is reinforced by the fact that Nyakomogendi, Mogusii's mother, is said to have led the people on their southward journey from Mt. Elgon.

Thus, Abagusii adopted their present name maybe at Kisumu, after all this is where the children of Nyakomogendi decided to move in search of good and cultivable land. It might be that not all people who came to be known as Abagusii were Mogusii's children, but they might have included all those people who decided to be under his leadership and follow him.

A critical analysis of the narration also reveals that after Masosa, the occupation of the Gusii Highlands might have been done in a rather haphazard way with different individual groups occupying certain sections. It seems that not all groups came back from Wire Hills to Masosa and then to Kabianga. We suppose that it is only the Sweta group and maybe some Abagirango who came back from Wire and thus went to Kabianga. Some people, especially the Abagirango, might have stayed behind and eventually became the South Mogirango, and some of them, according to some informants, moved to Mara in Maasailand. Here they named their children Momanyi[1] after the Maasai.

This is supported by the fact that the name Momanyi is widespread amongst the North Mogirango people. While the other sections which have this name may have got it through intermarriages with the North Mogirango people. It is further asserted that the name *girango* was adopted at Inani (a dense forest) which was said to have existed in present-day Bonchari (Wanjare). It is said that when the Abagusii went hunting in the forest, a certain group of people refused to kill the leopard and thus they were called *Abagira engo* ("refusers" of the leopard - *Abagirango*).[2]

This is more a support for the view that after Masosa, the Abagusii went southwards to Wire Hills in South Nyanza. It might have been during this southward movement that they entered the forest (probably Nyangweta forest). Therefore "Mogirango" was not really an ancestor but it might be referring to that period when the people now called Abagirango adopted their present name.

Using his family genealogy as a basis for reconstructing Abagusii history, Kiriama (1986), however, argues that by the early years of the 17th century, the Abagusii had not yet moved from their original cradle land. That is, if it is assumed that the first ancestor, whom Abagusii call, Banto (people) represents the period when man was created. At the time of Banto, the Abagusii and all the

---

1   **Editor's Note:** Abagusii refer to the Maasai as *abamanyi* (plural) or *omomanyi* (singular).

2   **Editor's Note:** there are other accounts of the origins of this name. e.g. *Ebimanyererio bi'Abagusii: Totems of Abagusii of Kenya*; (Nsemia Inc., 2024).

other people associated with them had not contemplated moving from the cradle land and therefore the Abagusii had not become a distinct group as we know them today. They were part of the large congregation of people who were later to separate and become distinct groups. Kiriama further argues that, if the claim by the Abagusii that they were twins with Mogikoyo (the eponymous founder of the Agikuyu) and Moragoli (eponymous founder of the Abamaragori) is accepted, it then follows that by the early 17th century, the eponymous founders of these respective groups had not been born and thus they were one people.

The genealogy as constructed by Kiriama (1986:192) indicates that Mogusii may have been born around the mid-17th century. Within one century, however, the Abagusii (descendants) of Mogusii had become a distinct group that had already reached their present homeland. This supposedly fast movement of these people makes Kiriama argue that this may be an indication that not all the people who now claim to be Abagusii are descendants of Mogusii. Some of the people might have come from different places and joined them at later stages during their migrations. Secondly, the name Abagusii might have been adopted quite recently; maybe after all the other related people such as Maragoli and Agikuyu had separated.

Thus, those people who decided to remain under the leadership of Mogusii were referred to as his people — Abagusii. Thirdly, Kiriama argues that if by the mid-18th century, the Abagusii were already in their present homeland, then their cradle land was not very far away, or their movements were fast and their sojourneys in the various places were very short indeed. If we take the first one to be true, we can argue that the cradle land was somewhere in northern/southern Uganda and this enabled them to reach their present homeland within one century.

It is further argued that the genealogy shows that the Abagusii did not occupy their present homeland as one corporate group but as individual groups and that occupation was haphazard, with some groups going southwards while others went northwards. Kiriama further argues that the present social-political-economic organization of the Abagusii was not adopted somewhere else and then brought into the present homeland but evolved in the present area as the conditions demanded. The fact that the Abagusii were moving from place to place in search of land suitable for cultivation shows that the Abagusii were not pastoralists as has been commonly held but were mixed farmers who emphasized the cultivation of grains which they supplemented with limited livestock products (Kiriama 1986).

Archaeological Work in Gusii Highlands

The first extensive archaeological work in the Gusii Highlands was first carried out by John Bower in 1971, who recorded over forty sites with material in a stratigraphic (original) context. The next work was done by Herman Kiriama in 1994. Bower recorded two pottery traditions which he named Kisii Soft Ware (KSW) and Button Necked Pottery (BNP) respectively (Bower 1973). The same pottery traditions were also recorded by Kiriama in his subsequent work. The KSW is crudely made, and thick-walled, the outside surface is poorly finished and the decoration is confined to either the rim or it is placed immediately below the rim of the vessel. The decoration includes nicks and notches on the rim, applique rows of notches below the rim, applique comb stamps, horizontal grooves and a row of punctates.

Button Necked Pottery (BNP) unlike KSW, is made of a hard compact paste and has an abundance of iron ore. Most of the vessels in this group also have a well-finished exterior. The decoration of this group consists of horizontal or applique buttons on the junction of the neck and shoulder or slightly below it.

Most of the BNP vessels were found together with the KSW vessels. This however, does not confirm or deny the contemporaneity (that these vessels may have been made or used at the same time) of these two groups since the sites from which they were found had been disturbed by modern human activities, especially farming or road construction. According to Bower, the KSW is the older of the two, dating to between 140±170 (about 80 CE). Bower, had argued that the BNP was only found in those areas that are west of the Manga Escarpment. The work by Kiriama however, found sites associated with the BNP on the eastern side of the escarpment as well. If the dates Bower gives are to be believed, then it is reasonable to assume that the KSW was succeeded by the BNP in most if not all areas of the Gusii highlands.

It is important to note that other than the pottery, stone tools were also found together or near the KSW pottery. The stone tools were found in the following sites, Magombo, Nyaisumi, Enamba and Nyairicha.

What is Heritage?

Heritage is the amalgam of all inherited traditions, monuments, objects, and culture. Cultural heritage can, therefore, be defined as those things and elements that a community or society inherits from past generations. Not all heritages of past generations are "heritage"; rather, heritage is a product of selection by society.[1] Cultural heritage includes both tangible objects (such as buildings, monuments, landscapes, books, works of art, and artifacts) and intangible elements (such as folklore, traditions, language, and knowledge). In most of Africa, there is no distinction between cultural and natural heritage because these tend to influence one another. For instance, a landscape that can include a forest, cave, rock, or waterfall which are natural phenomena can also be culturally significant to the community; people can go there to pray and because of this cultural act, the site will be revered, and respected by the community. Therefore, the cultural belief in the sacredness of the natural landscape or landform will ensure its preservation.

Tangible heritage is split into two groups, namely movable and immovable heritage. Immovable heritage includes buildings, landscapes other historic places and monuments. Moveable heritage includes books, documents, moveable artworks, machines, clothing, and other artifacts that are considered worthy of preservation for the future.

Intangible heritage on the other hand is those ideas and memories or the non-physical aspects of a particular culture such as stories, music, dance, language, traditions, and customs that exist or are maintained by the social customs of a society to enable members to identify themselves; that is to know who they are. It should, however, be noted and as it will be shown in this book, that as there is no distinction between natural and cultural heritage, it is also difficult to distinguish between intangible and tangible cultural heritage. This is so because intangible heritage gives live to tangible heritage. For instance, it is the belief and customs about the sacredness of an object that ensures its protection. For example, a community will believe that a certain waterfall or mountain is sacred because it is the home of their ancestral spirits. As a result, this tangible object will be protected because of this belief (intangible).

Heritage points to the past and shows how a society has developed. It helps in examining the history and traditions of a community and enables a community to develop an awareness of itself. It helps a community to understand and explain why that community is the way it is. It should be pointed out here that in this book we shall not be talking about Abagusii culture, but their cultural heritage. Culture is based on what people create – in other words the ideas, customs, and social behaviour of a particular people or society. It includes all aspects of the way of life of a people and includes human values, beliefs, customs, languages, and traditions. Culture does and can influence individual ideologies, and the social conscience of people. The diffusion of other different cultures can also influence a given culture. Consequently, people complain about the loss of cultural identity due to the emergence of new pop culture through the assimilation of other cultures. Heritage on the other hand is what the people inherit from past generations. Thus, when culture is subjected to change over time, the past attributes of that particular culture become a heritage. Heritage is important because it shapes human cultural identity, making heritage an integral part of humanity. Heritage can be summarized as what the past has given to us, what is valued in the present and what should be preserved for future generations. Thus, heritage not only includes aspects of culture, but natural and other societal aspects as well.

Cultural Heritage Protection

The pressures of modern development, such as the need for electricity, good roads and houses, and other amenities of modern life, have meant that heritage places have been destroyed or are under threat of destruction to give way for the construction of these amenities. For future generations to enjoy this heritage, there is a need for its protection. Protection of cultural heritage refers to all measures taken to safeguard cultural property against damage, destruction, theft, embezzlement, and any other forms of loss. This includes the prevention of the looting or destruction of cultural sites and the theft of works of art from churches and museums, all over the world, and measures regarding the conservation and general access to our common cultural heritage. Legal protection of cultural heritage comprises several international agreements and national laws, and these must also be implemented.

Much of heritage preservation work is done at the national, regional, or local levels of society. Various international, national and regional laws and conventions govern heritage. The most common international laws include the Convention concerning the Protection of the World Cultural and Natural Heritage (commonly known as the World Heritage Convention) which was passed in 1972 to govern the protection of tangible cultural heritage. The other is the 2003 UNESCO Convention on Intangible Heritage which governs the identification, preservation and management of intangible heritage. Other than these two, several other conventions and regimes govern the protection of heritage in the world. At the national level, each country has its laws for the protection of that country's heritage resources.

Care is usually taken to ensure that these local legislations do not conflict with the international laws on the protection of cultural heritage. In Kenya, the law that protects heritage is the National Museums and Heritage Act 2006. This law stipulates how to recognize an object or place as having heritage value, and how to declare a site as a national monument. It also designates the National Museums of Kenya as the custodian of heritage sites in Kenya. The problem, however, is that this legislation as that in most other African countries is based on the colonial legal system and ignores indigenous heritage protection or management systems. The result of this is that the local communities tend to feel left out from their indigenous heritage, and thus in most cases tend to disrespect or in some cases destroy the heritage places and objects as it no longer have any attachment to them. The result is the loss of important heritage places and objects and the disorientation or loss of identity by communities which no longer have a point of unique referral to their past.

Precolonial, Colonial and Post-colonial Heritage Protection in Kenya

Before the coming of the Europeans to Kenya, the different Kenyan communities had their local ways of protecting and managing their heritage places that involved elders and/or chiefs who looked after significant heritage resources within their communities. As already stated, these heritage resources could be anything that the community considered to be sacred and this could be forests, caves, open ground or mountains, or any other object that the community used to connect with their ancestors and therefore define the identity of the community. This local management system ensured that these places and objects were jealously guarded and passed on to future generations. At the onset of colonialism, however, this system was rejected and instead an alien Western management system was put in place. As a result of this colonial interference, currently, there are no heritage sites in Gusiiland that have been identified as national monuments, despite the recognition of such sites by the local community.

Colonial Heritage Management

In 1927, the Kenyan colonial government passed the Ancient Monuments Preservation Ordinance to protect coastal monuments. The 1927 Ordinance was replaced in 1934 by the Preservation of Objects of Archaeological and Paleontological Interest Ordinance until 1983 when it was repealed. The Ordinance authorized the governor to bestow a protected status on any monument or relic.

The first postcolonial heritage legislation in Kenya was enacted in 1983 when the Antiquities and Monuments Act (Cap. 215) and the National Museums Act (Cap. 216) repealed the 1934 Ordinance on the Preservation of Objects of Archaeological and Paleontological Interest. This Act provided a framework for the control of antiquities and monuments in the country. In 2006, these two Acts were consolidated into one: the National Museums and Heritage Act of 2006 (Cap. 295). Just as was the colonial and the 1983 legislation, the 2006 Act still views Kenya's cultural heritage as consisting only of tangible elements that include archaeological resources, cultural sites and landscapes, monuments and artifacts and gives a government entity, the National Museums of Kenya, the power of identifying, protecting, and managing a heritage place and removes the local community from managing their heritage places. As a result of legislation such as these that legislate how a site should be recognized as a national monument, most important heritage places in Gusiiland have not been recognized as such. The result is that sites that have been important to the wellbeing and identity of the Abagusii people have been destroyed and/or continue to be destroyed.

Chapter Two

Selected Gusii Heritage Sites and Places

Introduction

Since the 1970s, the use of heritage place inventory, at times known as cultural resource site survey, enables the preliminary appreciation of any cultural resources present in a particular place (Bronson & Jester, 1997). The term place includes a site, area, landscape, town, building, or group of buildings, which may contain components, contents, spaces, and/or views. Heritage inventory has been described by Pearson & Sullivan (1999) as a tool used to document the extent of cultural evidence present in a single small or large historic place. It includes all relevant written and graphic information on the evidence of heritage places and objects.

According to Australia ICOMOS (2000), it is necessary to document and assess the information relevant to a place to establish the whole significance and importance or values of that place. It has been noted that societies confer various values on their significant heritage places or objects. These values include cultural, religious, economic, social, educational, scientific, aesthetic, political and many others depending on the existing circumstances of that society. The knowledge and values of the community are therefore important ingredients in understanding the importance of a particular heritage place or object. These values and their assessment, however, are based on western paradigms and which unfortunately are being transposed to Africa.

For this book, however, to understand how Abagusii determined significant heritage places and objects, it is important to understand the Abagusii worldview and how this worked. In some places, these non-Western worldviews have been called traditional or indigenous perspectives or social values. Because the term *traditional values* have been inappropriately used to mean "backward, primitive or uncivilized", in this book, we will instead use the term *indigenous knowledge* to refer to the Abagusii method of conferring significance to their heritage places. Such indigenous knowledge has information that could change the way we think about indigenous cultural landscapes, cultural heritage, and the conception of "intangible heritage" (Sinamai 2021).

In many non-western societies, the indigenous systems of heritage governance are a "knowledge-practice-belief complex... that include the worldview or religious traditions of a society as well as the unwritten corpus of long-standing customs" (Jopela 2018: 55). In other words, the designation of a place or object as an important heritage is done within the whole amalgam of the religious, political, and economic setting of the society. That is to say that the guardianship of such places or objects will be firmly anchored in the intangible heritage of the community; the stories, events and personalities remembered through such stories. For instance, as we shall see in this book, the Abagusii considered a place to be of religious significance because it was believed that the place was able to connect the community members with their ancestors. However, when these stories are lost, a place/object loses the significance that emotionally attached the people to it and therefore that place/object becomes unimportant (Sinamai 2019).

Consequently, to guard against this loss, some rules and regulations governed behaviour in relation to a particular place. Heavy penalties befell whoever did not adhere to the prescribed rules and regulations. Since such places are important for conserving the history and identity of the Abagusii as a people, there is a need to not only document these places but also to put in place an effective and sustainable management program for these places. This is the reason why we undertook this exercise of documenting these places with the firm believe that making the values that the community attached to these places known, will spur movement from the authorities especially the county governments of Nyamira and Kisii to come up with strategic mechanisms for the management of some of these places. It should be noted that the 2010 Kenyan constitution devolved the management of cultural heritage places to the counties and therefore it is the responsibility of the indigenous authorities or grassroots groups to work with the county governments to protect the community's heritage places.

It should be noted that Kenya still has only one tier of heritage sites that are designated as national monuments by the National Museums of Kenya. There is still no requirement for the registration and protection of sites of local importance. It behooves the county governments therefore to pass local legislation that protects their important heritage resources.

It is also important to note that other than satisfying the social-religious needs of the local community, if well managed and presented, these sites can become a source of cultural heritage tourism (heritage tourism) that has been defined by the National Trust for Historic Preservation in the United States as "travelling to experience the places and activities that authentically represent the stories and people of the past and present." The visitation to these sites can be a source of revenue for the community.

It is worth noting that to Abagusii as in other African communities, the valuation of a heritage place is not confined to a particular place where that site is found, but its significance extends to the entire landscape. The issue of the nature of landscape, that is whether landscape is physical, natural, or just a cultural construction, has been debated by scholars since at least the nineteenth century when German geographers and French historians studied landscapes not just as "nature, but as the product of a long process involving people and natural circumstances" (Fowler 2004, 15). For example, Alexander von Humboldt (Ermischer 2004, 371) defined landscape as the "totality of all aspects of a region, as perceived by man."

In other words, other than their physical nature, landscapes represent some of the processes that have taken place in an area. Therefore, landscapes are an embodiment of the values, symbols, and meanings that societies have bestowed on them. Landscapes can therefore be said to provide both continuity and a sense of the passage of time. Therefore, through landscapes, it is possible to know the histories of people, places, and events that have taken place over time. A landscape is thus like a storyteller who has within his story the "lives and times" of those who have passed through it and played a role in its formation (Ingold 1993, 152–153).

Consequently, a cultural landscape is a place full of memory; it is "a surface that is full of historical signs and stories that are meant to strengthen, direct and validate both personal and collective memory of its places" (Raivo and Antonnen 2004, 4). Within Eurocentric scholarship, it is generally understood that "landscapes reflect human activity and are imbued with cultural values. They combine elements of space and time and represent political as well as social and cultural constructs of the people. As societies have evolved, and as human activity has changed, heritage places have acquired many layers of meaning that can be analyzed through historical, archaeological, geographical and sociological studies. The nature of the landscape is therefore a reflection of the values of the people who have produced it, and who continue to live in it (Taylor and Lennon 2011).

According to Taylor and Lennon (2011:3-4),

> "cultural landscapes are an imprint of human history. They can tell us, if we care to read and interpret them, something about the achievements and values of our predecessors. In this way, cultural landscapes are symbols of who are and can serve to remind us of the past. Because they are a record of past and present actions, cultural landscapes are a product of change. They embody physical changes which in turn reflect evolving attitudes towards the landscape. We must learn to interpret cultural landscapes as living history and as part of our national identity. They contain a wealth of evidence of our social and material history with which we readily associate heritage values."

It is a reality, however, that the phenomenology of landscape means that different cultures experience their landscapes differently, but again it is such landscape experiences that define what a cultural group chooses to keep as cultural heritage. Thus, the experience of the Abagusii people of their landscape is different from their Luo neighbours. We shall see this distinction for example when we look at the landscape of the Kisii soapstone; their Luo neighbours who may have occupied some of these heritage resources experienced it in a different way from the Abagusii. It can thus be argued that in Africa, the landscape is "cultural, it is performed, constructed, and venerated, and in return, it shapes people's ideas and philosophies" (Sinamai 2021:54).

The examples we will use here will agree with Sinamai's (2021:55) assertion that "in African philosophy, the landscape is not only alive but [is] also experienced sensorially, imagined in various forms of consciousness and lived through the collective memory of those experiences". Also, as shown by Kiriama (2021), landscapes can be imagined and experienced through imagined identities. It is within this context of people being located within specific landscapes (Kohn, 2013) that we shall be discussing the various cultural heritage sites of Gusiiland.

Cultural Sites

There is a belief that heritage places or objects have inherent values that need to be discovered and assigned specific levels of significance. This book, however, using examples from the Abagusii community will show that values are not inherent to heritage but are a construct of the community. A site is seen as having a cultural value if it has a full range of cultural significance as epitomized by the people. According to Mason (2002), there is no internationally agreed typology of cultural values. The aesthetic, historical, scientific, social, and economic values are the criteria adopted across many parts of the world for assessing local heritage places and providing guidance at the local entry-level. These are the criteria that we shall use to understand how the Abagusii people understand, classify, and appreciate their heritage places.

The Burra Charter, a document on how to classify heritage (Australia ICOMOS, 1988, 2013, 1999), sees cultural significance as a mechanism that assists in assessing the value of places and thus can provide knowledge on the history of the heritage and enable long-term appreciation of that heritage by future generations.

The significance of heritage sites is well recognized when it comes to open spaces; which though they have no built physical structure, have however, been instilled with significance because of the activities that are carried or used to be carried out there (Kiriama and Onkoba 2020). There are several such open places in Gusiiland; places where currently no activities are going on there, but which are imbued with significance because of their past activities. These places are both in the low-lying areas, Mountaintops or hills and specific places in existing rivers.

The Mountains

From the earliest times, mankind has looked to the heavens for answers to the mysteries of life. The early communities believed the heavens to be the home of the gods and natural phenomena such as the sun and the moon, rain, thunder, lightning, rainbows, and clouds were manifestations of the gods. The highest mountaintops on earth became the final height to which man could reach and be close to the gods while remaining within earthly bounds. For many communities, therefore, the most symbolic aspect of a mountain is the peak because it is believed that it is closest to heaven or other religious realms.

Consequently, the sacredness of mountaintops was knitted into stories of the gods in every community. The mountaintops had become sacred because that is where the gods were perceived to dwell. For instance, Mount Meru (Sanskrit/Pali) also known as **Sumeru**, **Sineru** or **Mahāmeru**, in India is the sacred five-peaked mountain of Hindu, Jain, and Buddhist cosmology and is considered to be the centre of all the physical, metaphysical and spiritual universes (Huntington 2003). It is perceived by the Asiatic people as being a cosmic mountain which is described to be one of the highest points of planet Earth and is the centre of all creation. In the Hindu religion, it is believed that Mt. Meru is home to the gods Shiva and Parvati. Also, in Indian classical mythology, it is believed that the sun, moon, and stars all revolve around Mount Meru. Folklore suggests the mountain rose from the ground piercing the heavens, giving it the nickname "the navel of the universe."

The Agikuyu people of central Kenya believe that God, *Ngai* or *Mwene Nyaga*, lived on Mount Kenya when he came down from the sky.[4] They believe that the mountain is Ngai's throne on earth. It is the place where Gĩkũyũ, the father of the community, used to meet with God. Thus according to the Agikuyu mythology, Gĩkũyũ is the first human being on Earth to ascend the mountain. *"Mwene Nyaga"* also translates as the "Owner of the Ostriches" or "Owner of the white patches (snow) on top of the mountain. Mwene Nyaga can also be translated as ostriches or white patches. Furthermore, the snow (in Kikuyu: Ira) caps of the mountain symbolize a crown on God's habitation. Agikuyu used to build their houses with doors facing the mountain. The Agikuyu name for Mount Kenya is *Kirima Kĩrĩ Nyaga* (Mt. Kirinyaga), which translates as the mountain that has the "Nyaga" – "the one with the ostrich." The Agikuyu attributed an ostrich's likeness to an object that was dark in colour with white patches. The name *Kĩrĩnyaga* therefore figuratively means "the one with white patches," referring to the glaciers on the several peaks of the mountain. The mountain, therefore is locally accepted as "God's Resting Place" or "Where God Lives."

Whereas, according to the Maasai, their ancestors came down from Mount Kenya at the beginning of time._The Maasai name for Mount Kenya is *Ol Donyo Keri*, which means "mountain of stripes", referring to the dark shades as observed from the surrounding plains. _A Maasai prayer referring to Mt. Kenya and the neighbouring hills and mountains states:

> "God bless our children, let them be like the olive tree of Morintat, let them grow and expand, let them be like Ngong Hills like Mt. Kenya, like Mt. Kilimanjaro and multiply in number."

Furthermore, Mount Ololokwe, also known as Ol Donyo Sabache, is a beautiful rocky mountain that suddenly rises from the vast plains that surround the Isiolo-Marsabit area. The mountain is sacred to the Samburu people who live in this region. Due to its perceived sacredness, the Samburu also consider Mount Ololokwe sacred because it provides food and water for the people and their livestock. They also use the mountain for prayers during drought seasons. Menengai Crater one of the biggest craters in the world has a lot of tales and superstitions among different communities such as the Maasai and the Kikuyu. The local inhabitants believe the mountain harbours evil spirits that lure people and animals to their deaths. Some people claim that the spirits are so strong that if you walk or pass a certain point of the mountain, you will fall into a trance. These events and stories earned the mountain the name, *"Kirima Kia Ngoma"*, which means "the mountain of demons." According to the Maasai, the Menengai Crater is haunted because of an inter-community war they had during the pre-colonial era. Two Maasai clans were fighting for the rights to the mountain pastures and areas adjacent to the Crater. One group won by throwing the others over the cliff of the mountain into the crater. Therefore, according to the Maasai, the rising hot steam that is seen on the mountain's top are the spirits of these dead morans trying to make their way up to heaven. However, in recent years, some Christians defy the scary stories the mountain holds and instead use the mountain for prayers and religious pilgrimage.

The Geology of Gusiiland

The Gusii highlands is a sub-mountainous landscape, shaped by deeply weathered Pre-Cambrian volcanic rocks of the Bukoban system within the Nyanzian and Kavirondian rock systems and consists mainly of basalts and basaltic tuffs, quartzites and cherts, rhyolites and tuffs, porphyritic and non-porphyritic felsites and Andesite. The Bukoban non-Porphyritic basalts are exposed west of Kisii town, they are fine-grained and grey-blue to greenish. The Bukoban quartzite and cherts outcrops can be seen along the Manga Ridge, North of Kisii Town. They are fine to medium-grained and white-bluish. They are believed to be a result of a sedimentation process in shallow water. The Bukoban andesite and felsites overlay the quartzites, they are fine-grained with a deep red or purple colour.

The Gusii highlands have one of the oldest rocks in Kenya with ages over 2,500 million years. According to the Kisii District Environmental Assessment report (1981), Nyamira county consists of the Bukoban, Granitic, Nyanzian and Kavirondian (Ablum series) types of rocks that form its geological base structure. Bukoban system rocks predominate this area and are called the Kisii series. The Kisii series consists of three divisions, that are the lower and upper divisions, and the quartzites that separate them. Though the Bukoban rocks were formed during the Precambrian era they are, however, much younger as compared to the Nyanzian and the Kavirondian systems. As a result of their ejection through the crust during the Precambrian age, granite rocks are also found in some areas because of either through original intrusive or as the product of granitization. The report further shows that whereas the Nyanzian system of rocks is made up of very thick lava flow, they are associated with variable thicknesses of prodastic rocks and lenses of conglomerate that include sediments and ironstones. The Kavorondian system of the Album series, on the other hand, consists of bands of grit or sandstone and mudstone with huge lenses of waterlain conglomerates.

The most notable features of Kisii County are hills such as Nyamasibi (2,170m), Sameta (1,970m), Kiamwasi (1,785m), Kiong'anyo (1,710m), Kiong'ong'i, Kiombeta, Sombogo, Nyanchwa, Taracha and Kegochi among others. While in Nyamira County the notable hills are Kiabonyoru (2,141m), Kebabe (1968m), Nyabisimba, Nkoora, Kemasare, Kiang'ombe (1,918m) and Manga Ridge (1,983m), among others.

Reverence for Mountains/Hills

As with other communities elsewhere in the world, the Abagusii also had mountains that they revered and held sacred. Within the Gusii highlands, there are five major hills (*ebitunwa*-pl; *egetunwa*-sing) which include Sameta in Bobasi Constituency, Kiabonyoru in Borabu Constituency, Ensaria in Bonchari constituency, Ribencho in Bomachoge Chache Constituency and Emanga which stands astride the Kisii-Nyamira common border. These hills have been sacred and each of them is believed to have its own unique attributes that make it stand out. To stress the sacredness and significance of each of these hills, songs, sayings, and proverbs were composed to praise them.

For example, when the elders blessed children or young people for good deeds done, they would say, "*Ochie kare buna Emanga n'Esameta*" (May you live long like the Manga and Sameta Hills). The implication here is that these are the oldest hills in the land, and therefore if one were to live for long; it should be as long as the two hills stood within the Gusii landscape. Nobody of course can say how old the hills are, but the argument is that these hills were found here when the Gusii ancestors arrived in the area and they have never reduced for even an inch, and, therefore they must have certain characteristics that have made them endure the passage of them.

These two hills have therefore been infused with the significance of longevity and good deeds. One who does good is assured of acquiring such traits as these hills that will ensure that he/she lives a long and fruitful life.

Originally, many of these hills were covered with indigenous vegetation. They were also habitats for diverse wild animals and birds of the air and were also a source of building materials like grass *(ekenyoru)*. As the name of the grass suggests, it etymologically originates from Kiabonyoru hills (a source of *ekenyoru*).

Each of the five major hills had unique attributes that were known in the length and breadth of the land. It was believed that Kiabonyoru stood tall and proud because of its height. It is from this belief that Abagirango (a clan that resides in the current Nyamira County) not far from Kiabonyoru was given the monicker "*Ching'ereru chia Bogirango*" (the proud and stubborn sons and daughters of Bogirango). Manga Hill is known as the hill of love. It acquired this reputation because Abagetutu, the most populous clan that settled there was peaceful, loving and accommodating. They are called "Abagetutu Enda y'Enchogu" (meaning they are as large as an elephant's belly) due to their renowned spirit of welcoming strangers to their midst.

Ababasi, the predominant clan around Sameta, were thought to be calm and had traits of being as innocent as young kids. Thus, Omogusii said, *"Babasi imbanga bana,"* meaning Ababasi behaved gently.

Ensaria Hill, found in Bonchari constituency equally had its own reputation. People who lived around Ensaria loved music and dance. It was from this area that most annual communal and cultural celebrations started. Such celebrations included circumcision (*ogosara*). The Gusii forefathers famously sung, *"rigereria Nsaria morore buna ekoyunga* (face Nsaria and see how it is burning)". This was about the celebratory mood that the people around the hill were always identified with.

Around Ribencho Hill in Bomachoge, there are two clans, Abakione and Abatabori. Ribencho Hill is not far from the Kisii-Narok common border.

The Narok side is occupied by the Maasai community whom the Abagusii refer to as *Abamanyi*. In the past, there was a dispute between these two clans (Abakione and Abatabori) on who should claim ownership of the hill. This often degenerated into a fight. Subsequently, there was a saying amongst the Abatabori people that *"timokaga Mbamanyi, abaisia n'Okione yeonchoire erwane korwa Ribencho moino* (do not think they are Maasai warriors; those are Abakione warriors who have re-organized themselves behind Ribencho Hill to confront us)". Apparently, the Abakione warriors used to dye their heads like the Maasai warriors to confuse their adversaries, Abatabori. It is believed that *chinkororo* (a group of Gusii warriors) emerged from these skirmishes between these two groups. Later on, the *Chinkororo* (who majorly adorned Maasai warriors' attire to disguise themselves against their adversaries played a critical role in fending off Maasai attacks on the Gusii community.

Sameta Hill

One of the most notable topographical masses in Gusiiland is the Sameta Hill. Located in the Bobasi constituency, Sameta's summit is estimated to be about 1970 metres above sea level. The hill is covered with grass, locally known as *ekenyoru,* and used to be popular in roofing indigenous huts. The summit has also herbal and other types of indigenous tree species that have withstood destruction. The remaining indigenous trees indicate that the hill was home to several indigenous fruit trees that may have attracted diverse fauna. The Sameta hill also boasts of deposits of soapstone whose amount has not been scientifically quantified. Ironically, the soapstone rock has survived for a long time because people around it do not have the skills to exploit it. The Sameta hill is also significant to the local people due to its spiritual value.

The spiritual significance of Sameta emerges from two caves that are found next to the soapstone mines. According to local tradition, the caves were the holy abodes of their ancestral spirits and therefore they were considered sacred. According to traditions, it was believed that the ancestors used to light a fire inside the caves to warm themselves at night. Therefore, to show reverence to the ancestors, one had to follow a well-laid-down procedure when going into the cave to either pray or thank the ancestors for answering one's prayers. This included making a knot of the *ekenyoru* grass next to the cave and then throwing pieces of dry wood into the cave. It was believed that the ancestors could use the firewood to light the fire at night to warm themselves. Failure, therefore, to deliver firewood when visiting the caves would attract a curse whose remedy was offering a sacrifice to appease the ancestral spirits. No person wished to take that path due to the fear and intricacies involved.

The tying of the grass was believed to be a sign of tying the evil spirits that may want to follow one to the cave; these spirits were therefore left out there where they cannot disturb the ancestors.

It should be noted that the grass was not uprooted but the knot was tied to the grass which remained standing. Further by using dry firewood nature was not disturbed. Consequently, there was a close harmony between the people and the environment. This kind of religious ceremony enabled the construction of a narrative of community solidarity and raised awareness about the interdependence of human beings and the environment.

We can therefore say that the local community had what can be called an indigenous ecosystem management system which ensured that both cultural and spiritual values did not compromise the biodiversity values of the site (Shepherd 2004, Verschuuren 2006). Further, it can be said that the acts of tying the grass and throwing firewood are a recognition that the local people's perception of sacredness was not limited to the caves alone but extended to the wider landscape. In other words, among the local Gusii people, the entire landscape of Sameta Hill was permeated with spiritual significance.

The forms of community-based precautions are not only limited to Sameta Hill but are found in many other places in the world. This is because sacred places are powerful and sometimes were perceived as having elements of danger, invariably they evoke complex cultural protocols and are always places to be respected. The ancestral spirits at sites such as Sameta Hill and many other places we shall discuss later were considered guardian spirits that ensured that the characteristics of the place were maintained and respected.

Currently, the practice of visiting the Sameta Hill for prayers is however waning, though there are a few individuals who still go there to pray, but apart from taking the requisite firewood, quite often they do not tie the grass as previously done. Curiously though, there are ardent Christians who also go to the cave to pray. However the Christians do not take the firewood, nor do they tie the grass.

Next to the cave is a huge Rock known as *Rigena ria Nyasindake* (Nyasindake's stone). One side of the giant stone has a poorly lit cave. Local folklore says that a mysterious man known as Nyasindake and his wife Nyogora lived in the cave; nobody ever saw this couple though everybody in Sameta believed and still believes that indeed this couple existed.

It is believed that the husband had supernatural powers that he used not only to bless but also curse people who provoked him. It is believed that the couple used to light a fire in the evenings to warm themselves; with people who resided in clear view of the hill saying that they could see the fire at night. This reinforced the belief that indeed, the couple stayed there.

Unlike the sacred cave, a visit to Nyasindake's cave required one being led by sniffer dogs. The canines were supposed to clear the way by scaring away venomous snakes that were believed to reside along the path. However as with the sacred cave, when visiting this cave one had to collect pieces of firewood and deliver the load to the mysterious couple. One was required to drop the firewood at the cave's mouth. Interestingly, residents claim, that whenever one visited the cave the next day, they never found even one piece of firewood. It is worth noting that in the past, only adults were allowed to go to the cave. Such visits mostly occurred during dry spells, an indication that the visits may have been for prayers.

The Sameta landscape, just like the Tabaka landscape, has outcrops of the Kisii soapstone. Part of this outcrop especially those found within the boundaries of the late Mayieka Onywoki's land have art carvings in the form of crafted holes that have been done in the form of the *ajua* game (board game); this game is usually played by men after work and it is surmised that men who were looking after cattle may have etched the holes out of the rock to recreate themselves while looking after cattle that were grazing in the hills.

The rock art has stood the test of time and continues to attract many people, including foreign tourists. Archaeologists, however, have not yet agreed to whether these holes were consciously etched by human beings. It is unfortunate, however, that the rocks are also being destroyed by the inhabitants as they do not see any economic value. This has stemmed from the fact that the authorities in charge of heritage management have not used this site in such a way that the locals receive benefits from the site. Indeed, some of the local people argue that they should preserve the site since the rocks are not edible; consequently, they rather sell them (rocks) and buy food.

A view of lower sides of Bobasi from Sameta Hill.

These rocks in Sameta bear writings of some of the people
who have toured the area.

Some rocks with indated scribblings at Sameta area of Kisii County.

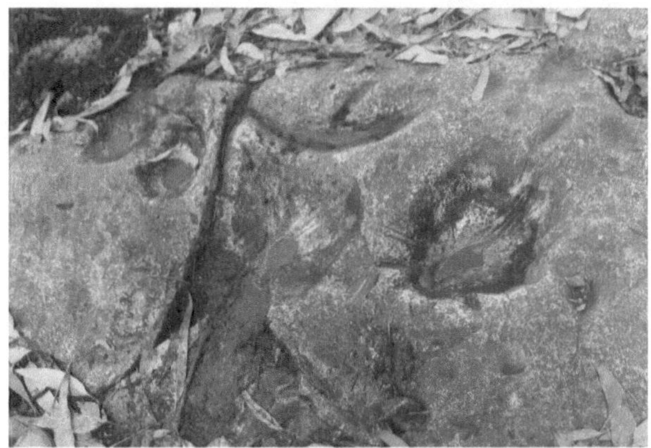

Creativity on display in Sameta area. This work is undated.

Most indigenous vegetation has been destroyed at Sameta Hill.

Some of the remaining thatching grass (ekenyoru) on Sameta Hill.

Works and destruction of Sameta Hill's scenic beauty.

Scattered soapstone at Sameta Hill.

An elderly woman at her home that was built after flattening a rocky section of Sameta Hill.

One of the soapstone quarries in South Mugirango Constituency.

Soapstone is a highly dependable resource in Kisii.

Soapstone quarry.

Remains after excavation of soapstone for carving.

The quarry also offers a fascinating view of places yonder.

A view of lower villages of Gusii to Bobasi side.

Kiabonyoru Hill

Located in Nyamira County, Kiabonyoru Hill stands at over 2000 metres above sea level, making it the highest hill in both Nyamira and Kisii Counties. As indicated earlier, among the Abagusii and indeed many other African communities, the deification of hills and mountains was part of their indigenous culture. In this regard, Abagusii held the hills within the borders in high regard and veneration.

Other than being the source of River Gucha, Kiabonyoru is known for other reasons. For instance, during drought, members of clans residing around it used to converge at its summit for the rain dance. The dance, popularly known as *Ribina,* was performed by elderly mothers. It was meant to appease the gods to allow the rain to come and end a persistent drought that threatened the existence of the people and their animals.

Local folklore has it that within the Kiabonyoru community, there lived a unique person whose name was Iriasi (Elias). Iriasi's sex was not known, though it is said that he may have been a hermaphrodite. He was believed to possess unique powers, including forecasting when rain would return.

One day, Iriasi is said to have joined women at Kiabonyoru Hill during a rain dance. As the dance hit the climax, heavy dark clouds gathered, and the gathering dispersed. Everyone hurried homewards. Something strange then happened. Some young men were curious to know the sex of Iriasi. Their intention was to have intercourse with Iriasi so that they could have a story thereafter. Their plan did not go as they wished. Instead, Iriasi violently rebuked them and left them while announcing that the village should brace for heavy torrential rains. True to his word, as soon as he vanished, there was a heavy downpour that caused flooding and damaged a lot of property including the death of many domestic animals.

Kiabonyoru is the highest point in Nyamira County. It is also the source of River Gucha, which is the longest river in Gusii region.

Kiabonyoru initially had a lot of grass (ekenyoru) that was used to thatch traditional huts. Most of the grass has since been destroyed.

Ensaria Hill

Ensaria Hill is found in Bonchari Constituency in Kisii County. It is located about 5km from Suneka Town. The hill was previously thickly forested and was home to diverse wild animals and birds of the air. It was also believed that the forest harboured evil spirits. The spirits resided in caves found in sections of the hill and specially the spirits protected the forest from any destruction as a result of human activities.

The Abagusii held Ensaria in high veneration. They considered it holy and only went there to seek blessings and ask for forgiveness and appeasement of the gods. However, the Gusii people believed there was a Supreme Being whom they called *Engoro*. There was an intricate procedure that one followed whenever he or she got to the caves. As in other locations, this entailed gathering dry pieces of wood that one dropped at the caves for the spirits to light a fire in the evening and warm themselves. There is a story being told that in the 1980s, a woman who ignored this procedure was once confronted by a mysterious being. Members of the community state that the two had a conversation that went like this:

Spirit: "Why didn't you come with firewood?"

Woman: "I did not have any," replied the frightened woman. In a nick of time, the mysterious woman" returned to the cave. This cave was close to *Rigena ria Kwamboka* (Kwamboka's stone). It is claimed that, after some time, the spirits moved from Ensaria forest in broad daylight. Several local people still claim to have seen them. It is surmised that the spirits may have been offended by this dishonour and why they decided to move out.

It is interesting to note that of the main five Gusii hills, it is only at Ensaria that people still go in their numbers up to this day to speak with their God. A majority of those who go for worship are Christians drawn from various Christian denominations. For instance, while visiting the area, the researchers encountered Pastor Robert Nyagosia of Eli-Shaddai Church who had been at Ensaria for three days and he had four more days to go. According to Pastor Nyagosia, the hill gives him a conducive atmosphere to make a special conversation with his God away from other people including his family. He claimed that he had been to the hill with the mission of prayer before and whatever he prayed for he got answered by God. This includes praying for the sick to get healed. Pastor Nyagosia recalled that many Christians before him had been to Ensaria Hill, and they got their prayers answered.

Within the forest, each worshiper selects his or her special point to pray. Some pray close to or on stones while others kneel under trees. One who declined to give us his name had prayed since morning and during our visit, he had taken a nap on *Rigena ria Kwamboka* (Kwamboka's stone). He was at ease, deep in sleep, his head resting on his Bible.

He said that he had isolated himself to pray because he was looking forward to entering the Kingdom of God on the second coming of Jesus. To him, he was walking in the footsteps of Jesus, who went to the mountains to make special prayers. However, he indicated that not all prayers need to be made from the hill. He first evaluates the problem at hand before he decides to either pray at home or go to the hill to speak to his God.

According to this individual, *Rigena ria Kwamboka* was holier than any other place within the forest. He claimed that he had prayed there before and seen God's hand. He informed us that one of the notable prayers was his recovery from a disease that nearly took his life. He indicates that before coming to the hill, he had been to various hospitals but when he was told that he needed to pay Sh300,000 to undergo surgery, he decided to look for an alternative since he could not raise the amount. That was how he ended up in the forest and after days of intense praying and fasting, he was cured.

Next to *Rigena ria Kwamboka* is *Rigena Ri'erikoru*. The stone, according to Pastor Nyagosia, is a preferred site for a group of Catholics who visit the hill to pray. There was evidence of used candles; an indication that, indeed, such a group of worshippers had been there. Someone had also uprooted some herbs. This gives the impression that the hill has enormous significance to the people.

Ensaria Hill in Bonchari Constituency.

One of the individuals who was at Ensaria Hill for prayers.

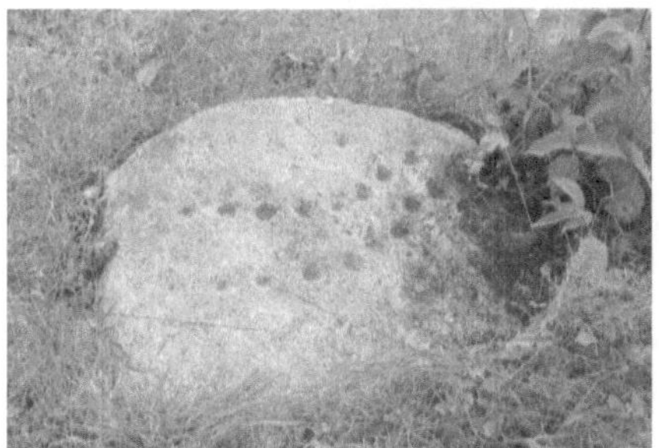

The perforations on the rocks are believed to have been made by traditional herders in Kisii.

These marks on the stone are a result of human activities that date back to hundreds of years.

This stone with a hole in the middle (ensio), formed part of water powered mills which were common in Gusii region in yesteryears.

A view of lower villages of Gusii to Bobasi side.

Rigena ria Kirera (Kirera's stone). Chief Kirera made strategic decisions and declarations from this stone.

Manga Hills/ Escarpment

It has already been mentioned that the Gusii community is comprised of a notably small number of people in comparison with other communities. The people used to move from place to place, particularly to find the most habitable region to settle. Top in their consideration was their personal and collective security, the security of their animals and an ideal environment devoid of severe diseases and flooding. It appears that when they finally got to the present-day Gusii highlands, they decided that they had eventually found an area that was quite suitable for final settlement.

It is worth noting that the Abagusii community continued to face frustrations fueled by their small number in a region surrounded by a relatively larger ethnic grouping; the Maasai, Luo and Kipsigis. These communities were considerably big and never shied away from confronting the Abagusii people by way of forcibly taking away their cattle and killing people in the process. As a result, due to security considerations, most Gusii families moved to relatively raised areas within their region. Most of them settled around Manga due to its high altitude.

Manga Ridge (*Emanga* as known in Ekegusii) which has an elevation of 1983m above sea level, provides one of the most fascinating sceneries in Gusii land. It cuts through Ikuruma, Itibo, and terminates at Mote Momwamu near the current Kisii Town. The summit is presently punctuated with several trees and some grass. There have been attempts to excavate gravel, particularly from Mote Momwamu side and this is progressively destroying the scenery. This is unlike in the past when it had plenty of grass that made Abanchari (one of the Abagusii clans that live in the current Bonchari constituency) and overlooks the cliff to say, *"Tangori Emanga ebe eyaito erinde indisie chiombe* (I wish Manga was ours so that we could graze our cows there)."[1]

The Manga Ridge forms part of the common boundary between Kisii and Nyamira counties. The lower part of the cliff is in Kisii while the upper part is in Nyamira.

From Manga, Gusii warriors could see their adversaries advancing from the distance and quickly prepare themselves for a face-off. This could sometimes end up being bloody, but not to the extent it would have happened if the warriors were caught unaware.

However, it is worth noting that, in recent years, confronted with population pressure and disregard for the beauty of heritage, Manga is progressively losing its scenic beauty. To an outsider, Manga might appear to be just another simple natural feature but to the locals, its importance is as immense as their history.

1 **Editor's Note:** other versions of this exist such as, *Omochari igo akorera buna otangori Manga nseito, anga tinaranda buna emurwa,* meaning that "Omonchari says wishes that [the] Manga [Ridge] belonged to them so that they could spread like Napier grass." This and all other variations of the same underline the significance of the Manga Ridge.

The people talk nicely about the escarpment that acted as a shrine, entertainment site, administrative and refreshment spot over the years.

Sadly, at present, there is massive quarrying at Kiabiraa and Mote Momwamu. Some sections of the hill are now bare due to increasing erosion. At sections like Kiong'anyo huge cracks emerged after prolonged rainfall in 2019. This has caused fear to people staying near the escarpment making many of them temporarily move out of the area.

A view of Manga escarpment from Motemomwamu area.

Excavation of building materials at Manga escarpment.

Residents climb a rocky path
at Manga Escarpment.

The oldest court in
Manga, Nyamira
County.

At the time, locals claimed that they noticed a black thick substance in the cracks. They called for researchers to step in and find out if they were residing over an active volcano. So far, it is not clear if there are experts, especially geologists, undertaking the study, as much as it is quite significant to avoid future calamity. With the surging population and crowded settlement, perhaps such a study will give a glimpse into foreseeable and unforeseeable activities that may or may not affect the future of the settlers.

It is important to observe that away from the picturesque and breathtaking scenery that the Manga escarpment provides, the area has a relatively big contribution to the survival of the Gusii people. The contribution is in various spheres: social, cultural, economic, and political. In other words, there are stories within this unique phenomenon that go beyond the broader story of Manga. Several of the tiny stories that form part of the bigger story are shared in the following sub-sections.

Igena Ria Mengere (Mengere's Stone)

One of the unique rocks along the Manga Hils is *Igena ria Mengere* (Mengere's Stone). This rock sits at the edge of one of the ridges. According to folk history, in the past there existed a man by the name Mengere whose name the rock is named after. However, we could not find sufficient detail as regards the origin of the name of the stone.

The Catholic Church has built a residence for the Carmelite Nuns about 100 metres from the site while a huge cross stands next to the rock. Occasionally, gospel musicians visit the sites for video shooting. Just like the ancestors of the Abagusii people, Christians hold the place in high esteem. The Catholics do special prayers there. Apart from Our Lady of Mercy Mount Carmel Chapel, the church has also built St Joseph's Prayer House in this area.

According to the local people, *Igena ria Mengere* was a hide-out for community members during an impending attack from their adversaries. Once they stood on top of the stone, they could see their enemies from faraway and take cover while strategizing on how to defend and launch a counter-attack. At the same time, young men looking after cattle could shelter under the rock from rain or sunshine.

Furthermore, it is not known exactly when it happened, but members of the community are said to have discovered that there were some spirits underneath the rock and thereafter the community developed a belief that such spirits influenced both their collective and individual lives. People subsequently started to offer prayers at the rock so that the spirits could safeguard them from trouble and bless their land. Members of the community came from far and wide to perform special prayers at the tip of the unique stone with a belief that it was an abode for their ancestral spirits.

This culture of convening at Igena ria Mengere for prayers still goes on but in a relatively different form. Curiously at present, the prayers are made by Christians, particularly Catholics. Christianity is a different religion from the community's ancient beliefs and practices. The ancient worshippers seem to have been torn between worshiping their God in heaven and the ancestral spirits that they believed resided at the place.

In Mathew 14:23 (NIV), it is written that Jesus prayed in the Mountains. This implies that such raised geographical features were regarded highly even before the Bible was written. Mountains are often seen as a site of revelation and inspiration. For example, in the Bible, it is written that the covenant to Moses was revealed at Mount Sinai by God. The mountains therefore serve as places of revelation and transformation alongside being attraction sites for tourists and pilgrims.

Mountains, and in our context hills/cliffs/ escarpments, are the ultimate symbols of stability and virility. When Jesus speaks of mountains being moved or even being more dramatically "thrown into the sea," as a result of faithful prayer (Matthew 17:20; 21:21), he is deliberately invoking an impossibility as far as humanity is concerned. There is the overwhelming power of "God on High", the Supreme Being who had control of all things, the living and non-living.

Christians continue to perpetuate the culture of regarding particular places as ideal for special prayers and fasting. For instance, the Catholics in this region, see Manga Hills to be an equivalent of Mt. Camel. However, it is interesting to note that the nuns who have a residence next to Igena ria Mengere mainly stay within their compound and can hardly be seen mingling or interacting with members of the immediate community.

In recent years, Igena ria Mengere is one of the key natural features that attracts the interest of foreign tourists whenever they are in the Kisii region. According to the local people, a Canadian once visited the area and spent several hours at the stone. The tourist, according to our informants, had read the story of Manga Hills in a newspaper. When he visited, he spent not less than two hours at the stone. His notably long stay in one spot attracted the curiosity of some members of the community who wanted to understand his intentions.

During his two-hour stay, the tourist reportedly took several pictures, stretched himself on the stone and eventually scooped some soil and uprooted some grass. He packed the items in a small bag and then took more pictures with community members. At the end of it all, he inquired if the land belonged to a particular person.

Manga Hills is gazetted as government land set aside for posterity. Under this, it should be fenced up and its boundaries clearly demarcated. This is not the picture that one gets on the ground. The area has been massively encroached in recent years. Although some of the trees in the area belong to the County Government of Nyamira which is the custodian of the land, some of it is cut by local people for personal use. This, alongside the breaking of rocks for building materials, negates the intention of setting the area aside as protected land.

Igena Monto and *Ajua*

Another notable feature is *Igena Monto*, loosely translated as "a stone that looks like a human being." The stone, they argued, looked like a static human being from a distance. It was at a place where two footpaths tend to appear atop Manga cliff. Anyone approaching it, particularly, for the first time could only be surprised that he had been wrong when he got close to it; that is, the stone appears as a figure of a human being from far.

Roads, including the Kisii-Nyamira highway, Manga-Mote Momwamu Road and many others around Manga were until recently not there. Therefore, people used to take shortcuts through the bushes whenever going to the lower or upper side of the cliff when travelling to places such as present-day Kisii, Nyakoe, Magombo, Ting'a, Kebirigo and Nyamira townships. For this reason, *Igena Monto* became increasingly popular since it featured all the time one sought for direction. Over time, the rock has been broken and lost its shape and size. One wonders if it will not be flattened altogether someday, given that there have been no efforts made to preserve and protect it.

Close to *Igena Monto* herdsmen whiled their time playing *ajua* (bao game). Many people know *ajua* as a game that employs a wooden board that is about six feet long and 48 seeds of the wild orange tree. The game, considered to be complex and strategic is played widely in Eastern Africa. Presently, the game is most popular along the coastal region and people who are good at it are held in high respect. The game is dying out in Gusii, although one can find elderly men playing it outside small shops and kiosks in market centres such as Ting'a and Rwora.

It is however worth noting that one did not necessarily need a wooden board to play *ajua*. At Manga, Sameta and Got Chaki Hills, this game was played on a flat stone that had requisite "holes". At Manga, the holes are in two rows with ten holes on each side and two holes at the end of each section used for the accumulation of one's "earnings" in the game. The two-row bao game is characterized by the capture of seeds (or stones) from the opposite side of the player's holes and also by the capture of holes by the two competitors and subsequent use of these captured holes for the profit of the new owner.

The alignment of the Manga game is north to south. The local people believe that the "trough" (as the bao game is known in the region), was incised, miraculously, by the ancestral spirits. It is also believed that the location of the game is the same spot where the ancestors also sharpened their farm tools such as machetes, hoes and knives. However, to archaeologists, the incisions became more pronounced over time through natural corrosion. Additionally, in the olden times, men sharpened their farm tools using the same stone.

Next to the bao game, there were special indigenous tree species (*emetaburo*) whose branches served as "toothbrushes" for the local people as they relaxed on an open space nearby that was covered with smooth grass.

During the time of this research, it emerged that the *ajua* trough had been destroyed and the indigenous trees had also been replaced by exotic species like blue gum (eucalyptus).

Although the Abagusii play the same game today, the modern ones are carved on wood. There are, however, some people, like the Pokot who still play the game on boards made of grounded boulders (Townhead, 1979). Other examples of stone game boards have been found associated with prehistoric sites such as the Neolithic and iron using the site of Hyrax Hill in Nakuru County and near Nakuru City (Leakey, 1948).

None of the current occupants of the area seem to know the origin of these holes. One elder told us that his grandfather had told him that it was God who had given the game to his ancestors. From archaeological and historical evidence, this area was occupied by the present settlers possibly around the late 17th and early 18th centuries CE, which means that the holes may probably be more than 250 years old.

Igena Monto/Igena Mu

Photo Courtesy: Charles Tinega

Ngora a Mwaga

If there is a cave in the whole of Gusii that is crowded with stories told in different versions, then it is *Ngora a Mwaga*[2] *(hole of the ancestral spirits/or the abode of spirits)*. This is an overhanging cliff on the central edges of the Manga Ridge. It is known as *Ngoro a Mwaga* because of two holes (fissures) that are found around it and whose end is unknown. One hole is slightly above the other. Locally, it is believed that the holes comprise male and female figures and terminate at Lake Victoria. Other versions argue that the holes are bottomless.

The locals claim that they used to hear the voices of various animals and people coming from inside these holes late in the evening, especially when the chicken went to roost. Further,

2   Editor's Note: *Ngoro a Mwaga* is a shorted form of *Ngoro ya Mwaga*.

other people who went to the shrine claimed to have seen a bright fire at night. These incidents have been attributed to the spirits that are supposed to have inhabited these holes. Some people, however, argue that the voices may have been echoes of the hens, cows and the people who live in the vicinity of the area. The voices are no longer heard and this has been attributed to the infilling of the holes which has been done either deliberately by the landowner, or by erosion.

Not everyone approached *Ngora a Mwaga*. Those who visited the "shrine" did so for special reasons. This included praying and appeasing the ancestral spirits and seeking forgiveness and blessings. One had to approach *Ngora a Mwaga* circumspectly per the dictates of the ancestors.

As said elsewhere in this book, the major event that earned *Ngora a Mwaga* a special place in the history of Abagusii was the *Osaosao* battle that happened in the 1890s between the Abagusii and the Kipsigis. It is said that before the war, Nyakundi, who was known for spell-binding curses in the interest of the community, in the company of the community's great prophet Sakawa, proclaimed *Ngora a Mwaga*, a proclamation that eventually led to victory in the community's battle against Kipsigis warriors.

Like other venerated places, there was an intricate and clear procedure that one followed whenever approaching *Ngora a Mwaga*. The ritual included putting grass together and knotting it before one could gather a few pieces of wood and throw them into the hole to appease the ancestral spirits. It was believed that the ancestral spirits used the firewood to light a fire and warm themselves at night. As a result, firewood never accumulated at the entry of *Ngora a Mwaga*.

It is worth noting that even today, nothing has changed as this procedure is concerned. At any given visit, one's tour guide will disclose that the procedure should be adhered to. *Ngora a Mwaga* is a very popular attraction and one would expect that since the firewood has been thrown into the dark hole since time immemorial the hole should have gotten full by now. But this is not the case.

People performed rituals at the shrine. Some prayed to be blessed with children, while others prayed that their newborn babies be protected from any harm and evil. It was also common for people living in outlying villages to pray or make particular invocations while facing the cliff.

It is believed that no living person has ever entered or emerged from *Ngora a Mwaga*. Its reputation as the home of supernatural powers has kept many at bay who would dare enter there. Despite the beauty of this place, no one charges visitors to take a tour. It can be argued therefore that this is one of the untapped or unexploited tourist sites that can fetch revenue for the local people and the county government. Sadly, at the moment of writing this book, there was evidence of increasing destruction of areas adjacent to *Ngora a Mwaga* through the mining of stones for construction, and the clearing of indigenous vegetation.

Construction Industry: *Samuel Ondari crushes gravel near Ngora ya Mwanga in the Manga Escarpment.*

Image: Magati Obebo. *The Star Newspaper,* 15 November 2021

Egetii kia Angwenyi (Angwenyi's Field)

Apart from spectacular mountains and forests, the African people also confer significance on other places such as open fields where important ceremonies or events take place. One such field in Gusiiland is *Egetii kia Angwenyi* or Agwenyi's field in the Manga area. During the colonial era, colonial chiefs reigned over large areas and wielded a lot of power and influence. Below the colonial chiefs were their assistants as well as village elders. Above the chiefs were the Divisional Officers (DOs), District Commissioners (DCs) and Provincial Commissioners (PCs), respectively. This administrative structure stayed in force until Kenya promulgated a new constitution in 2010 that ushered in devolved governance; but the basic governance structure, previously known as the Provincial Administration still exists albeit with weakened authority. In other words, the "defunct" Provincial Administration represents the National Government down to the village level and is expected to work in harmony with the current county governments. As such, occupants of some of these positions in the national government structure as per the 2010 Constitution acquired new titles, while others retained the old ones. Those who retained the old titles include chiefs and their assistants.

Central Kitutu Location was one of the locations under the then Kisii District (now Kisii County, one of the 47 counties in Kenya). The area under Central Kitutu now comprises the Kitutu Chache South and Kitutu Chache North constituencies of Kisii County and the Kitutu Masaba constituency of Nyamira County.

Kitutu Central Location stretched from Ekerachuoki (the current Kisii-Homa-Bay border) to Ekenagwa (the current Nyamira-Kericho/Bomet border). Up to 1948, its chief was Ooga. Upon Ooga's exit, his son Zacharia Kirera Angwenyi ascended the throne. Angwenyi, being the son of a colonial chief, was among the few young men from the Gusii community who had obtained formal education. This had earned him a job as a clerk based in Kisii Town, something that had given him exposure and made him well-grounded to serve in his new position as chief.

Due to his distinct administrative style, Chief Zachary Angwenyi became one of the most famous Gusii men and women who have since died. But even in death, he continues to be venerated due to the good work and the wise decisions he made. After his demise, tens if not hundreds of boys across Gusiiland were named after him. Within Gusii culture, it should be appreciated that no parent would dare name his child after someone who led a crooked life and did not leave a legacy behind.

One of the major socio-cultural factors that Chief Zachary Angwenyi remains known for is the landmark ruling that he made on dowry negotiations, payment and eventual marriage.

Previously in Gusiiland, a man who was ready to marry had to pay bridewealth of at least twenty heads of cattle. This became an unwritten "rule" that was universally accepted in the community, and nobody was ready to go against it. However, it should be appreciated that the economic well-being of families was not at par. Twenty herds of cattle, therefore, was not a small number, particularly, for the poor young people. It was therefore noticed that since at the time no parent would let his daughter leave his homestead before he received dowry, many suitors shied away. This situation left many young men who could not raise the dowry with no other option other than remaining bachelors for a long time.

It was against this backdrop that elders within the community got alarmed and had their heads thinking. They approached Chief Angwenyi at his Manga home with their concerns; that there were many young men who, even if given all the time in this world, could not be able to raise the requisite dowry to enable them to marry. This was a serious matter, for it meant that the community's population would stagnate or grow at a notably slow pace since very few men would manage to marry.

Outside Angwenyi's residence, was an open field measuring about two acres. Next to it is a section that has huge stones. It is said that Chief Angwenyi preferred to sit on one of these stones when seeking counsel from community elders. Sitting at the stone gave him a fascinating view of the lower side of his area of jurisdiction and the hills yonder in Homa Bay County. He could

Children walking homewards on Egetii gia Zakaria (Zachariah's field) in Nyamira County.

also see parts of Kisumu Town and Lake Victoria. Equally, he enjoyed a cool breeze, all these giving him an ideal atmosphere to think wisely.

It was at this site that, after listening and consulting with the elders, Chief Angwenyi made a landmark pronouncement. He directed that henceforth, dowry be reduced from 20 to 6 heads of cattle. He further directed that the heads of cattle should include a bull, *eeri y'egesicho* (for procreation). The offer of the bull, according to Angwenyi, was an indication that the groom's family had given the dowry in good faith and the two families involved meant well for one another and would maintain the new bond of relationship into the future.

This ground-shaking pronouncement was received with acclamation, particularly by young men as well as parents whose sons could not afford the dowry of 20 herds of cattle. So happy were his people to the extent that they decided to preserve the field where the pronouncement was made as a sacred place. Many others named their sons after Angwenyi while others composed songs in praise of him. Below are lines from one of the songs composed in this regard:

"Zachariah ore bw'Ooga (Zachariah the son of Ooga)

Agakuma chiombe (Set dowry)

Isano n'eno na eeri y'obokombe (at six cows and a bull)

K'enywomo yagasinya (When marriage had become hard)

Ko'bamura bakanywoma (Then young men married)"

It is several years since Chief Angwenyi died but he continues to be venerated across Gusiiland. The field in which he made the ruling is still intact. However, it should be noted that by the time of undertaking our research, the field did not have a fence. Further, according to Morara Angwenyi, the son of the late chief, he is considering establishing a cultural resource centre and hotel that would ensure the continuity of the Gusii heritage that is disappearing. However, Morara noted that his attempt to start a cultural home some years back was frustrated after some unknown people torched the few huts he had built.

The River Systems

Water has always been central to human life. The earliest prehistoric hunters and gatherers, although nomadic, also settled down along rivers, lakes, and coastlines to ensure access to crucial resources, particularly water. Later, many prehistoric farming societies manipulated water systems and redirected water to meet their essential needs. Ancient states managed water resources with large-scale facilities such as aqueducts, irrigation systems, and boulders. People used water to cultivate the earth, for drinking, food, and agriculture.

Consequently, river systems are other important resources that inspire and encourage people to connect with their river heritage and share in its safekeeping. Rivers as heritage sites are therefore integral to the health, well-being, and identity of the current and future generations. Free-flowing rivers such as those found in many parts of Gusiil form the foundation of local cultures and communal grounding, and have enormous ecological significance, as they serve as the critical sanctuary for diminishing freshwater resources. Water sites such as rivers, lakes and coastlines form heritage spaces that are closely linked to traditions, rituals, and narratives. The maritime heritage is spiritually significant to local coastal communities in Eastern and Southern Africa (Sharfman 2017). The heritage sites form important sources of knowledge both for recognizing how water systems worked in the past and understanding their impact on the present cultural and economic systems.

Some researchers have examined some elements concerning the management of the water heritage. For instance, Christer Westerdahl, a maritime archaeologist, introduced the notion of maritime cultural landscape to name, and better explore, study, and preserve existing cultural networks present between communities based on travel and trade over water, be they oceans, seas, inland lakes, rivers, and artificial waterways. These networks included social and political relationships as well as associated ancient routes, harbours, shipyards, settlements, and other physical structures (Westerdahl 1992). The Ramsar Convention, an intergovernmental treaty for the preservation and wise use of wetlands, covers the natural and cultural heritage of wetlands (Ramsar 1994). In addition, UNESCO's World Heritage Center has published a special issue, *Living with Water* (2011) which elucidates on socio, economic and political impacts of existing water bodies and adjacent communities. The International World Water System Heritage Program, launched in 2016 by the World Water Council in collaboration with the International Commission on Irrigation and Drainage, has initiated a comprehensive register for the intangible values of water-related heritage.

People understand rivers in various ways, and usually, people who live close to rivers develop unique characteristics associated with living along those water resources. River management therefore comes as a reaction to several social and economic issues, including water resource usage, energy production, river basin management and transport. Water-related cultural heritage resources are defined as expressions of people's thoughts, beliefs and religions that value the complex relationship with water rather than humankind's physical relation to the water bodies and surroundings, as individuals or as communities. Therefore, water-related cultural heritage resources are those movable or immovable objects, sites, structures, groups of structures, and natural features and landscapes that have archaeological, paleontological, historical, architectural, religious, aesthetic, or other cultural significance (van Schaik et al.2015).

In this cultural context, the question that was foremost in the minds of the Gusii people was how to protect the whole river ecosystem and at the same time use the river resources to create wealth and social value. There was therefore critical need for cultural re-appropriation of the rivers and developing a sophisticated knowledge of the river environments. Subsequently, the rivers were treated as an interconnected system; that is, one river will be either a feeder/tributary or the taker of another river's water. The rivers, therefore, form whole ecosystems which are linked to the lives of the people who inhabit areas adjacent to them.

River Gucha and other Tributaries

The major river system in Gusiiland is Gucha. In most literature, River Gucha is also referred to as River Kuja. It should be noted that in the Gusii dialect, the letter "j" does not exist. This error happened at a time when those who documented physical features like rivers, hills, forests, and boundaries of clans in the Gusii region relied on spoken interviews since their respondents could not read or write. It should thus be appreciated that the name Gucha etymologically emanates from the root word,

Egucha. Furthermore, Gusii highlands are traversed by other perennial rivers which flow westwards into Lake Victoria. Among the notable ones are Mogusii, Riana, Mogonga, Eyaka, Risonto (Sondu), Chirichiro, Nyabomite, Echarachani and Iyabe Rivers.

Permanent rivers such as River Gucha have, for many years been used for fishing activities, while waterfalls at Keera in Chitago Borabu can be used for various forms of water sporting activities if well planned and developed. In addition, landscapes such as Kegochi, Kionganyo, Igoma, Keboi, and Sakawa hills among others that are adjacent to the rivers are unique landforms that can be used for hiking activities.

The Gusii people understood rivers as an interconnected system. For this reason, they had several proverbs/sayings to underscore this specific fact. For instance, in cases of rivers such as Gucha and Omogonga, which meet near the current Ogembo Township, the Gusii people believed the two rivers usually fought at the confluence, and that because of their strong currents and even though after joining together they became one river. Omogonga is the victor (i.e figuratively as it were as the waters of Omogonga River overtook as it were those of the Gucha, and therefore the Gusii people would say, *Egucha noira nsisi Omogonga nokobua* (even though you stretch wide (referring to river Gucha) Omogonga surpasses you or *Omogonga no bikoro* (Omogonga is stronger). These sayings/ proverbs conveyed important cultural information to the populace about the various aspects of life and the need to respect one another, no matter one's standing in life. It can therefore be said that the Gusii people used water-related heritage to preserve and transmit various components of their cultural heritage.

The Gusiiland water heritage therefore holds significant folk histories of existing water bodies and safeguards their cultural memory for generations to come. It has been argued by some scholars that the study of water history and heritage can be a source of information, inspiration, and identity-building in water management and wetland recreation; they are important resources to the redevelopment, redesign, and reuse of existing and ancient water systems as well as for the design of new river resource use systems. The reuse, adaptation, or redesign of old water heritages can enhance the livelihoods of local communities, especially the local communities' sense of place and identity (Heine et al 2020).

Furthermore, the Gucha River System which starts as a small spring at the foot of Kiabonyoru Hills comprises of River Sare and River Gucha. The Gucha River drains most of the Gusii highland region and has several tributaries that include Enyangweta River whose confluence with Gucha River is at the boundary of Kisii and Migori counties, Omogonga River that joins the Gucha River at Ogembo Town originates from Ramasha and Masimba areas and Echirichiro River which drains from Keroka Town area and eventually connects with the Gucha River. The river is also joined by the Kemera River which starts from the eastern side of Manga Hills at Chabera market.

According to the local people, the water volumes of River Gucha have drastically reduced over the years. This is evidenced by dry depressions in which the water flows through before it forms one stream several metres ahead. The depressions were formed when the water volumes were bigger to the extent that people never crossed the springs even at their source in Kiabonyoru Hills, especially during rainy seasons. But because of human activities including cultivation for agricultural production and the growing of eucalyptus trees on the banks of the springs, the amount of water in the springs that are the source of River Gucha has declined drastically. For instance, one of our respondents, Alfred Mose, who at the time was 57 years old and who hails from Omomiso village near Kiabonyoru, recalled that when he was young, the area had plenty of water. At the time, youngsters learnt their swimming and fishing skills in the emerging springs. He further said that swimming skills were critical if one wanted to cross the springs from one side of the river to the other, especially during the high rain season. Those who did not know how to swim either used a longer route or got aided by skilled swimmers to cross the river. Presently, such skills are not necessary because the springs are too tiny.

River Gucha is significant to the people of Gusii and parts of Luoland. The river empties its water into Lake Victoria. As stated, the river originated from Kiabonyoru Hills in Borabu Constituency, Nyamira County. It then passes through West Mugirango and Kitutu Masaba (still in Nyamira County) before it crosses over through Kisii County. In Kisii, the river's course continues to swell as it meanders through Nyaribari Chache, Bobasi and Bomachoge constituencies and is joined by several springs before it joins Migori River and flows into Lake Victoria. The river passes at the heart of the current Ogembo Town, which is the Gucha Sub-County Headquarters, where, as stated earlier, is joined by River Mogonga.

As with mountains, rivers such as Gucha were considered sacred by the Gusii community. Rivers were thought to personify or to be abodes of ancestral spirits. Therefore, rivers could be used as cleansing sites such as ritualistic bathing and offering of sacrifices whenever calamity struck to appease the ancestral spirits. Consequently, the Gusii always paid attention to the behaviour of a river and its different stages. According to Gusii elders, River Gucha, used to swell and break its banks during heavy rains, particularly in April to May. During such times, the water swept makeshift bridges downstream and uprooted trees. People also drowned in the river, particularly those caught up in the rage as they crossed the makeshift bridges from one village to the other. Therefore, it was known that danger lurked at the riverbank whenever there were torrential rains. People, more especially children were warned to stay away. It was considered a bad omen for one to lose his life at the river. In case it happened, elders ensured that once the body got retrieved, it had to be buried at the riverbank, regardless of the distance to the dead person's homestead. After that, sacrifices were offered to appease the river spirits.

The Gusii people, and especially those who lived near the rivers, knew well that River Gucha or any river for that matter did not have a uniform depth. They knew that water moved slowest at the deepest section and fastest at the shallowest point. This was critical when it came to crossing the river. Shallow places had visible stones upon which one would step as he hopped and jumped to the other side of the river. This is how the people ended up knowing that specific points such as Endiba ya Nyankwana, Mochengo and Ndiba Ngare were the deepest sections of River Gucha.

Similar to its source, River Gucha has considerably shrunk in size downstream. The prevailing scenario is blamed on the increasing exploitation of the river and its riparian areas for agricultural production and other forms of economic activities. Due to erosion, the water is often dirty and contaminated. Effluents from sewer lines drain into the river and this has not made matters any better. Furthermore, due to pressure on land, people have built pit latrines close to rivers while others dispose of waste directly to the rivers. Farm inputs including fertilizer, animal and industrial waste equally find their way into the water. This has not only compromised the quality of the water for domestic use but also threatened aquatic life. The net effect of this is that the sacredness of River Gucha is no longer held by the local community and, therefore, it is treated like any other water source.

However, the river which stretches for over 160km from the source at Kiabonyoru to Lake Victoria has some enchanting scenes that can serve as tourist attractions. The scenes include Rianyakwana Falls in Bobasi constituency. The falls can also be utilized to generate electricity to serve the local communities. However, the increasing degradation of the water resource puts into question its sustainable utilization to improve the livelihoods of the local people.

A section of River Gucha during a rainy season.

A section of River Gucha.

This tree stands on the exact spot that acted as ancient court (ritongo) in Gucha, Kisii County.

The colour of the waters of River Gicha are evidence of pollution due to various human and natural activities such as soil erosion.

Chief Kirera's house was one of the kind, the first ever stone house in his home area.

Ogembo Court stands not far from the ancient court of Abagusii in Ogembo Township-Kisii County.

A modern court built and opened during the time of Justice David Maraga as the head of judiciary.

This facity was funded by the national government but it later on closed shop due to management challenges.

A portrait of Chief Zachariah Kirera, displayed by one of his sons.

Chapter Three

Gusii Indigenous Craft Industries and Rock Art

Tabaka Landscape

The Tabaka landscape found in South Mugirango Constituency in Kisii County is famous for the large quantities of soapstone, which is a metamorphic and hydrothermal rock consisting mostly of the mineral talc, which also includes sericite and kaolinite. Its development is linked to hydrothermally transformed lava, which explains its classification as a Pulferay. It is a relatively soft stone and very tactile. Hence, soapstone is soft and relatively smooth. It gives the stone a smooth feeling similar to the rubbing of a piece of dry soap on the skin. It is from this feeling that the stone derives the name "soap". While it can be found in other parts of the world, the Tabaka soapstone is considered unique and naturally comes in different colours. White and pink coloured soapstone is softer and easier to work with, while black soapstone is the hardest.

A rocky quarry in South Mugirango, Kisii County,

Although both archaeological and oral tradition evidence indicates that the soapstone industry in Gusii land dates back to over three thousand years it is however, not clear exactly when soapstone sculpturing started (Ochieng, 1974:4, Eisemon, 1988). The Tabaka landscape is made of several hills, each of which has soapstone outcrops. At one of these hills known as Goti Chaki, there is evidence of carvings and other forms of art made on the soapstone. Most of the rock art in the area features a geometric style consisting of concentric circles painted in red and white. S a rose flower. Some of the carvings tend to depict human figures but are relatively disjointed- that is, the head and the body are separate. This Tabaka rock art is thought to date back to between 700 and 1300 CE (Odak 1985). This rock art style is dominant in the Lake Victoria Basin. Other paintings include spirals, circular geometric patterns and unique spirals with rays.

Other rock engravings include "cupule" sites where cup-shaped depressions have been grounded into the rock surface. Although similar to those in Manga Hills, cupules often resemble a bao game, their original use is likely to have been for ritual purposes such as initiation. Cupules are thought to be amongst the oldest forms of rock art, in the world. This form of art is called Twa Art and is found in large parts of eastern and central Africa and is believed to be the work of a small hunter-gatherer community, possibly related to or are the ancestors of modern pygmies. The Wandorobo or Ogiek(Okiek) may also be partly descended from some of these people. A similar geometric style of art consisting of concentric circles has been found at other sites around Lake Victoria such as Mawanga and Kwitone in Mfangano Island in Homa Bay County of Kenya (Odede, et al 2014). Other rock art sites are found in Kikongo which is located on a rock above Royal Sukuma graves in the Mwanza region of Tanzania (Tanner, 1953: 62-7; Chaplin, 1974: 12), and Kakoro, Loteteleit and Nyero in Uganda (Chaplin & McFarlane, 1967:207-8; Chaplin, 1974:19).

It should be noted that Mawanga and Kwitone sites are the closest geographically to the Kisii rock art sites and they appear to have some similarities. The cave at Mawanga on Mfangano Island consists of several paintings that include concentric circles and spirals with rays. They are smaller than those in Kwitone and less dramatic but are executed in the same way and possibly belong to the same rock art culture. The Kwitone rock shelter, which is found in the upper parts of the Mfangano Islands on the other hand, has several paintings that consist of spirals, concentric circles and circular geometric patterns executed in red and white colours.

Chaplin (1974: 19) reported the presence of red ochre paintings at the top of Itone Hill on Mfangano Island. The paintings consisted of concentric circles, spirals, and stylistic "sun" figures. One of the "sun" figures was very elaborate and consisted of a flame-like drawing, imprinted on the outer perimeter of a series of concentric circles. The site was associated with supernatural powers and miraculous events by the residents. However, most of these rock art paintings are increasingly being destroyed by various human land use activities such as quarrying and agricultural activities.

However, the greatest concentrations of Twa paintings are found in northern Zambia, and the adjacent Democratic Republic of the Congo, spreading west into Angola, east into northern Mozambique and Malawi and then into East Africa. Currently, the Batwa people who are the originators of the Twa paintings live in Uganda and the Democratic Republic of Congo. There are now several interpretations such as the one which contends that the art is based on the astronomy of the Batwa culture while another interpretation is that these paintings were associated with some kind of ritualistic activities of the people.

It has been stated by Odede et al (2014) that the paintings at Mawanga and Kwitone still retain ritualistic powers in the culture of the Abasuba community. For instance, the Wasamo clan, who live around the Mawanga cave are the rain makers of the Abasuba, and the elders agree that the paintings have been used for rain-making ceremonies, with the red paintings representing the moon and the white ones the sun (Odede et al 2014:20). Shem Mogendi one of the carvers, states that the concentric rings which form a cobweb may have been incised by herders as they looked after their cattle at the hill. He further says that perhaps the rings, whose start and end one could not tell, meant that life is too complex, and no one can expressly say how it starts and ends; that they represent reflections on the puzzle of life. The artists may have wondered what life is and how it starts and ends.

It is important to state that the earliest known rock art in the Sahara region is about 7,000 to 12,000 years old. But the oldest scientifically-dated figurative rock art in Africa dates from around 26,000–28,000 years ago and is found in Apollo 11 cave in Namibia. The painting and engraving traditions in Africa developed over the last 30,000 years into a highly sophisticated way of expressing complex beliefs about the supernatural world. Consequently, African rock art is the earliest remaining evidence of spiritual/religious beliefs; they speak of Africa's rich history and culture, and a time long before writing was invented. It is still difficult to establish accurate dates for rock art. Scientists use radiometric techniques to date organic components found in the rock art area such as charcoal and date binders such as blood, egg yoke and urine. Furthermore, in some parts of Africa, experts have been able to develop chronologies based upon the existence of ancient species such as the crocodile and elephant, now extinct in the Sahara, or the introduction of exotic new species like the horse, camel, or dog. However, in the absence of associated material, it has been difficult to date the Gusii rock art.

Because Africa's rock art was developed in exposed places, much has now disappeared. What we see today was probably created during the last 12,000 years, while much of it is less than 6,000 years old. The Ajua game is common all over Sub-Saharan Africa, and this makes it ethnographically difficult to establish who were the original rock art carvers.

Next to the rock art at Tabaka, was a series of two-row bao games with a north-to-south alignment. Osaga Odak (1986) calls them cup marks, but their arrangement and resemblance with those at Manga makes us argue that they were bao holes.

Informants whom we asked about these two features said that God had put them there to be utilized for their ancestors. However, one informant thought that the ringed engravings were a result of people scrapping the soapstone to remove the powder which they then used to smear their bodies during ceremonies such as funerals and rain-making. But this explanation may not be true because the rings are done in such an orderly manner meaning that some other intention other than that said by the informant was meant. According to Osaga Odak (1986:2), the engravings represent the universe. According to him, the cluster of holes represents the distant galaxies, a concentration of stars. But as we have said before, the holes at Got Chaki compare favourably with those at Manga Ridge and elsewhere, and thus they cannot be said to be representative of stars. As we said above, the holes may have been used to play the bao game (ajua) and the different arrangement may have been due to different concepts of playing the game. It may be that the holes were made and used at different times hence the different arrangements. One thing common to all of them is that there are holes where one could accumulate their earnings- a feature that is common to all bao games.

For the engravings, one may postulate that they are a symbolic representation of the people's concept of life and death. The concentric rings may have been a representation of the journey that the deceased took after death. This is supported by the fact that the rings form a pattern that if followed, never arrives anywhere. It is like a puzzle, and indeed death is a puzzle to the living. When somebody dies, the living do not know what happens to him or where he goes. Thus the ancient residents of Got Chaki may have represented this dilemma in the art. This assertion is supported by the fact that some figures on the rock are shaped like humans but with the body and head separated. This may be a representation of the deceased. The people of Got Chaki may have believed that when one dies, the body is removed from the head, as the soul is believed to be removed from the body. One may thus conclude that the art is a representation of the ancient people's belief in the relationship between life and death. A representation of the people's concept of what happens after death. This a reflection of the belief that death is a puzzle and nobody other than God himself can understand it.

Although the Tabaka area can claim bragging rights as the home of soapstone, the resource is also available in Sameta, within the Bobasi constituency where as shown before, the *ajua* game has been carved onto these rocks.

Origins of Abagusii Stone Carving

It is not exactly known when formal sculpting of soapstone started among the Abagusii. According to various informants in South Mugirango however, the first carver was a young man named Nogori who had come to Bomwari village in the 1800s to herd livestock of one man known as Moseti. At the time, the fields under which the precious stone rested were covered with grass and thick indigenous forest. Both wild and domestic animals wandered freely in the pastures. As he was going about his job, it is said that Nogori picked a stone that impressed him. He therefore decided to use it to make a pipe to use for smoking tobacco *(etumbato)*. Tobacco smoking at the time was an accepted pastime of elders after work or while looking after livestock in the fields. Nogori liked his pipe and decided to share it with his boss, Moseti who was equally thrilled when he saw it. The excitement surrounding the product is said to have marked the beginning of the soapstone industry. In quick times, Nogori was able to make other items including a bowl and a pot (*enyakanga*).

The making of a pot out of soapstone marked an exciting turn for the Gusii community around Tabaka and beyond. Before then, the community relied on earthen pots that they purchased from their Luo neighbours. These pots were used for cooking and storing water for domestic use. They were happy that they now had an alternative source of these precious kitchen items not far from them. The soapstone pots were even more durable and became hardened when they were heated.

Moseti had hosted Nogori as a "shamba boy" oblivious of the innate capabilities the young man had. He quickly started to follow Nogori to the grazing fields to witness firsthand how the young man worked this magic stone. Moseti learnt the process and soon he made a jug (*mamboleo*) - a small water container with handles that were in the shape of human ears).

During that time, Kenya had become a British colony and the colonial government had posted a British District Commissioner in Kisii. When Bwana Hochi (as the District Commissioner was known by the locals), saw the soapstone containers, he purchased some items. This first monetary transaction which occurred around 1915 is important in the history of soapstone carving. Later other colonial administrators and travelers to Gusii land purchased pieces of soapstone sculptures and with time these sculptures became valued by visitors to Gusii. The colonial period therefore introduced the commercialization of soapstone. As a consequence, the Kisii stone was no longer merely an item for household utility; the production had shifted from the household to the commercial space. The Abagusii people now started to use the artifacts as currency to trade with their Luo neighbours in border markets like Riosiri, Nyamarambe, Rongo and others.

At the same time, the colonial government, to make the Kenya colony pay for itself, introduced taxes such as hat and poll tax that were to be paid by every male individual over 18 years. This forced men to move from their homes in such of jobs on white-owned farms. Moseti was no exception. His search for a job led him to Narok in 1917. When he returned home several months later, he was told that the colonial DC had paid a visit and that he wanted more of the soapstone products. Since Moseti was away and there was a major communication barrier between the white man and the natives, Nogori was afraid. In his mind, he imagined that the DC had planned for their arrest for destroying stones that belonged to the government. Amid this fear, Nogori fled from the village, never to be seen again.

It soon turned out that the DC was serious about purchasing many more soapstone artifacts from Moseti. After making a few items for the DC, Moseti was taken in the DC's vehicle to Kisii Town for an entrepreneurship seminar. On his return, he recruited like-minded villagers to make the soapstone items that were most preferred by the DC. Moseti's recruits included Ndege and Ong'esa (the grandfather of Elkanah Ong'esa), a renowned contemporary soapstone carver. The trio of Moseti, Ndege and Ong'esa started to carve earnestly. They could make the carvings in a group and then transport them to Kisii for sale. Villagers who had been disinterested bystanders gradually got drawn into the trade. They got the requisite skills to do the job and they never turned back.

The Gusii people have always been communal and to lessen the work burden, they usually called amongst each other to till the land, sow, weed and harvest as a group- a system known as *risaga*. This collective initiative was quite systematic. Moseti and his colleagues gradually transferred the *risaga* concept into the soapstone sector. Their decision was informed by the fact that the DC and his huge network of friends, relatives and colleagues had created a relatively huge demand for finished soapstone products. The market spread its tentacles to areas as far as Kisumu. The carvers needed to sustain the demand and there was no better way of doing it at that time other than pooling their skills together and working as a team.

To satisfy the Kisumu market, and since there was no motor vehicle transport, Moseti was forced to walk to Kisumu with his products. Movement particularly at night had been prohibited by the colonial government yet the transport network at that time would not allow Moseti to travel to Kisumu and back in one day. To solve this, he obtained a letter from the government, allowing him to spend nights at the homes of any chief in whose area of jurisdiction dusk found him on his way to or from Kisumu.

Since there was no formal art school in the area then and even now, the carving skills continue to be passed from generation to generation through apprenticeship although a few individuals have managed to make it a profession by attending training schools elsewhere.

Elkanah Ong'esa (2011), one of the most accomplished contemporary Gusii soapstone artists, has over the years managed to carve renowned sculptures including the *Bird of Peace* sculpture that adorns the entrance of the United Nations Educational, Scientific and Cultural Organization (UNESCO) Headquarters in Paris, France. Elkanah opines that the earliest forms of soapstone carvings were made before the Abagusii settled in their current homeland in the late 18th Century. He argues that the rock art at Goti Chaki was made by earlier people who were, probably, non-Gusii and that these were the original initiators of the soapstone art from whom the Abagusii people copied the art of soapstone sculpturing (Snarman, 1971).

A machine that was used to make chalks in Tabaka area in the 1980s. The dust chalks were used by teachers in the region and beyond.

A soapstone carver at a quarry in Tabaka area, Kisii.

KISOP was the company behind the making of chalks from soapstone in Tabaka.

Men at work at a quarry in Tabaka, Kisii County.

Some of the chalks that were made in the 1980s at Tabaka area of Kisii County.

This building housed the soap making and carving factory in Tabaka.

It is worth noting that the name Goti-Chaki in the Luo language means white hill and it has been argued that it is the ancestors of the Luo people who may have stayed here before the coming of the Abagusii and may be responsible for the rock art. However, the present boundary of the Luo and Abagusii is about 3km from the Got Chaki area. Other than Goti Chaki, other places in South Mogirango where soapstone rock art has also been found include, Bosinange and Nyabigena regions. Unfortunately, as is the case in the Sameta area, lack of conservation efforts and protection has seen these unique rock art carvings damaged and they have now disappeared from the various historical sites in South Mogirango and Sameta region (Ong'esa, 2010).

Farming activities, quarrying and lately road construction are the major threats to the Kisii rock art sites. Consequently, rock art sites at Goti Chaki, Nyabigena, Tabaka, Nyatike, Ibencho, Mote O'Nkoba and Keboye areas in Kisii have been destroyed due to human activities.

Got-Chaki Hill

Got Chaki Hill stands conspicuously tall in South Mugirango Constituency, in Kisii County. The hill is strategically placed and can be seen from as far as Nyabigege, Nduru, Bomanyama, Kiabigori and Riosiri. Residents of Rongo and Kamagambo in the neighbouring Migori County equally enjoy an exciting view of the hill.

According to oral tradition, before the Abagusii settled at Got Chaki and its immediate neighbouring villages, the hill was grazing fields of the Luo community. It is said that the name *Got is a* Luo word for hill and *Chak* is also a Luo word for milk. Hence *Got Chak* (Got Chaki). Hence Got Chaki means the "hill of milk." Folk tales say that cattle that grazed on this hill produced plenty of milk at the time.

Other sources, however, have a slightly different story concerning the name of the hill. According to Joseph Orina, the Luo community had figuratively named their Abagusii neighbours "Ja got", meaning people from the hills or people who reside in the hills. Due to distortion by Abagusii because of pronunciation, the name gradually changed to Got Chaki.

According to Orina, the Luo were not coerced or ejected from the grazing fields. Instead, they moved out voluntarily to settle in the low-lying areas of the present-day Migori and Homa Bay counties of current Luo Nyanza. Following the exit of the Luo from the grazing fields, members of the Gusii community gradually moved into it, intending to confine themselves together and make a close-knit community that would not be broken by their aggressors during cross-ethnic attacks that were prevalent at the time.

As already mentioned, Got Chaki was the most prominent rock art site in the area until the destruction of this site a few years ago.

Some markings on stones at Got Chak area of South Mugirango. The rocks were destroyed soon after this picture was taken.

The concentric rings art at Got Chaki

Cultural Significance

Soapstone has historically been intertwined with the cultural and religious aspects of the Abagusii people. Its religious significance was seen through its use in rites such as initiation (Onyambu and Akama 2018). The rock paintings and engravings of Goti Chaki have for example been said to hold ritualistic meaning for the community. In its powdered form, soapstone was used by the Abagusii people in sacred rites such as divination and healing (Ong'esa 2011).

The Role of Christianity in Advancing the Soapstone Production

When catholic missionaries came to Kenya and introduced Christianity, they came with plastic models of the nativity story as well as images of Jesus, the Virgin Mary, and angels. Multiple interviews on the ground indicate that this fascinated the creative minds of those engaged in soapstone at the time. The artists eventually sculpted similar models of the nativity set, the angels, and both the baby and adult Jesus, among other items. The missionaries were also fascinated with the soapstone carvings so they started placing orders for various items for their various institutions. For example, Tabaka Mission Hospital, a health facility established by the Catholic Church has at its entrance and other strategic places within the hospital, soapstone sculptures of various sizes. Some are in the "likenesses" of Jesus, the Virgin Mary, and the cross, among others. Such carvings are also found in other Catholic-sponsored institutions such as schools, colleges, churches, and hospitals.

Initially, the sculptures were in abstract form, but this changed to realism when the white missionaries brought their plastic, metallic and even wooden items and requested to have a prototype out of soapstone. The effect of this is that it killed creativity and instead introduced what can be termed as assembly line mass production. Large quantities of the same product, as demanded by the consumers were being produced. Since the consumer came up with the model of what they wanted to be produced, the artist no longer used his creative mind to come up with a product. This has in turn led to the lower prices of the products.

There are now two categories of artists. There are those in the value chain whose only motivation is to earn an income, while there are others who are there because of passion. The latter occasionally find it difficult to sell what they have made. This is due to the intimate significance they attach to their products. Such people who are driven by passion take a reasonably longer period to finish a project because they seek to give it the best by modifying and giving it a perfect finish. For those specifically looking for income, time is of the essence. They seek to finish the task ahead of them quickly to earn that cherished extra shilling.

Carvings of animals such as leopards, rhinos, lions, and leopards are some of the very popular items, especially with international tourists. Curio shops in major towns including Nairobi as well as within national parks, game reserves and museums equally stock soapstone products. There are individual and group traders who export the products to continents like the Americas, Europe, and the Middle East.

Carvers say that some tourists who have enough time to stay longer make special orders for items such as dolphins and whales. If the artist has never seen such an animal, he relies on plastic models or pictures that may be in the possession of tourists, the internet, books, and other sources.

The idea of *risaga* (working in a group) enabled more people to enter this value chain. They could come together, make items for a member for a day or two and let him sell the finished products as his. This way, some were able to build stone houses while others were able to take their children to school. Many others were able to pool money to buy cattle and pay as dowry, this being a token of appreciation that tied a marriage. However, to a large extent, the commercialization and the advent of middlemen have caused the collapse of *risaga* system. This has happened because each person wants to work independently and then jostle for buyers. This has, however, not helped individuals as they lack the capacity to access markets. Aware of the fact that as a united entity they can get better returns for their labour, some traders have structured and registered groups. Through them, they work together from the mining/ excavation, transportation to the shade, shaping, sketching, carving, sanding, painting/ polishing, packaging against a checklist and transportation to clearing/forwarding agent. Exports generate better returns than selling locally.

In the early years of the 2000s, a non-government organization known as SITE tried to make interventions to reverse environmental degradation and other negative effects of disorganized and unprofessional quarrying. The organization refilled several quarries and planted trees. Kisii University also sensitized residents on the importance of converting the quarries into fishponds.

To preserve the soapstone whose quantities are unknown, there is a need for the community and both levels of government (national and county) to place the resource where it deserves to be in terms of bettering people's lives and generating foreign income. Presently, there is a huge waste right from the quarries. This may be solved by the use of modern excavation machines like compressors, and cranes, and putting up shades for carvers to work under. The road network (there is tarmac around the quarries) should be enhanced so that vehicles can reach the mining sites.

After carving, leftovers should not be regarded as waste as they can be used to make terrazzo, a powder that is mixed with cement to give buildings a perfect finish. Presently, the powder goes for as little as Sh100 per 50kg bag at Tabaka. It is often purchased by traders who repackage it and sell it at Sh600 or more in towns.

Other products from soapstone include paints, floor tiles, and soles for shoes, chalks, shoe polish, mosquito repellents, insulators, soap, ceramic utensils, and pharmaceuticals among others. Unfortunately, no factory has been established in Tabaka and its environs to make any of these products. Instead, traders from as far as Nairobi and even Tanzania and Uganda come in with trucks, and carry the raw materials to their far-placed factories at exceedingly low prices. This leaves the owners of the resource wallowing in poverty as middlemen and brokers make millions and perhaps billions of shillings.

In the early years of the sculpture of soapstone, women were mostly bystanders and end users of the products. This was because mining and carving was and is still considered a male job. However, as time has gone by, it appears that women are making inroads in this male-dominated venture. Apart from excavation and transportation of the rocks to the workshops, women as well as young girls are now engaged in subsequent activities. These activities include sanding, painting, polishing, decorating, packaging, and dispatching the products to customers located in Kenyan towns and elsewhere in the world. One can say that women are allocated those roles considered not to be laborious.

At the same time, artists have carved thousands of sculptures that convey the message of love. These sculptures either tell the story of love between a man and a woman or a woman and her child. They often depict the firm embrace and tender care that is synonymous with women. Such carvings are a hot cake to most customers.

Soapstone Ambassadors

As indicated earlier, thousands of people work and depend on the soapstone industry for survival. Some especially artists, develop a near-intimate relationship with the rock once they have moulded it into an object they desire. Some of the artists who have gone on to become renowned world sculptors include, Elkanah Ong'esa, Hezbon Obara, Gerald Motondi and Joseph Orina.

Ong'esa is a professional sculptor whose works include the Bird of Peace which is on display at the UNESCO headquarters in Paris and the *Freedom Fight* which is found at the UN headquarters in New York, USA. In 1996, Ong'esa completed the *Bottle Dance* sculpture for the Olympic Games in Atlanta, Georgia. Another project, the *Dancing Bird*, is on display at the entrance of the American Embassy in Nairobi. He has also written extensively about soapstone.

Like Ong'esa, Gerald Motondi started off his sculpting at Tabaka, a skill he acquired from elderly sculptors. He progressively pursued a course in Fine Arts and has done notable sculptures that are found in several buildings across the world. Motondi has obtained recognition on an international platform for his creativity and focus. In 2002, his sculpture won a gold medal alongside an Olympic Torch in China.

For Hezbon Obara, the safety of amateur carvers and the preservation of the environment are issues he is passionate about. He has numerous photographs that tell the story of the damage that disorganized and unsystematic quarrying has caused to the area.

Joseph Orina, who was 70 at the time we interviewed him for purposes of this book, vividly recalled what happened in 1967. He was barely 16 years old at the time when he travelled to Nyeri with a friend to sell some carvings they had made. Once in Nyeri, they came across a government residential house and learnt that the occupant was a white man. They developed an urge to enter the compound but got hesitant at the gate. Why? The gate was clearly labeled, *Mbwa Kali* (Fierce Dog). Nevertheless, they marshalled courage and entered the compound, and they were gladly received. It turned out that the elderly *mzungu* had been to Kisii where he bought a few soapstone carvings which he held dear as souvenirs. He was also excited to see them with more carvings, and he gave them Sh400 in exchange. He also gave them an additional Sh10 for them to buy meat for Moseti once they got back to Kisii. This was a very huge amount of money at that time, given that a kilo of meat went for 70 cents. The youngsters left the home all smiles and returned to Kisii.

Soapstone Products

Soapstone Products

Iron Smelting

There are several traces of iron working around the Gusii highlands. These are in the form of slag heaps and tuyere fragments. The most extensive slag heaps were found at the current Nyamira hospital, Biego, Geseneno, Nyambaria, and some parts of Nyaribari Masaba. At Biego for instance, a total of five slag heaps, complete with tuyere fragments were recorded. Informants said that previously there used to be extensive ironworking in the area and that ploughing and the construction of a road that leads to the local primary school had destroyed most of the furnaces.

Furnace at Nyangoso Area

This was the only concrete evidence of ironworking that was found. This furnace was exposed during the construction of the road leading to Nyangoso Primary School. Unlike the other areas, there were no slag or tuyere remains on the surface. However, the surface outline of the furnace was made of bricks/or burned clay. The furnace had five tuyeres resting on the wall sides. The outer wall of the furnace was made of burnt clay with an inside lining of soft whitish clay. The bottom layer had a mixture of tuyere, slag and ashy soil. Most of the slags were soft and of poor quality.

From its morphology, this furnace may have been a free-standing bowl of medium height built over a slag pit dug into the soil, the only openings in the bowl being for placement of tuyeres on either side of the bowl at ground level. Informants told us that the Abagusii used such types of tuyeres.

Estimating that the furnace was of medium height, and the presence of numerous tuyere fragments, we can postulate that this furnace was bellow driven. It is hard to find evidence of the bellows as most of them may have been made of wood and may have rotten away. The reconstruction of the furnace can then be that it had four tuyeres, two on each side, which were worked simultaneously by two bellow blowers. The nature of the slag, soft, therefore showing some liquidification, indicates that this was a smelting and not a smithing site.

Ethnographic Evidence

Consequently, oral evidence collected in various parts of the Gusii highlands indicates that ironworking was a widespread phenomenon during the pre-colonial period. This spread may have been due to the localized nature of the smelting industry. That is each region had its iron specialists who catered for the area's needs. Some of the smelt iron tools that were in great demand included hoes, spears and bangles.

Iron smelting among the Gusii people was a family and male affair. A family affair in that family members helped the smelter collect the iron ore from its source and do the necessary preparations like washing and drying it before it was finally smelted. The best ore for smelting was obtained from the swampy areas, especially in Sironga, Nyambaria and Engenyi areas among others. The journey to the ore source could start very early in the morning and those involved including the smelter, his wife, children and any other member of the clan who wished to join. On the eve of departure however, the smelter and his entourage had to offer prayers to God (*Engoro*) asking him (God) to help them succeed in obtaining the best ore, have enough sunshine to dry it and, generally, bless the entire smelting process.

Once at the ore site, the men could do the digging while the women did the washing of the ore and packed it into baskets. Once at home, the ore was dried in the sun before being smelted. The time for drying depended on the nature of the ore and the weather. In good weather and if the ore was not so dumpy, it could take close to a fortnight to dry.

While the ore was drying, the smelter could be busy preparing charcoal to be used in the smelting as well as the ore smelting furnace. The furnace was a cylindrical clay wall measuring five feet high and a diameter of between six to eight feet built over a subterranean pit.

The furnace was usually located at a distance of about a mile or so from the village. This was partly to avoid "evil" eyes as well as women who were supposed to pollute the smelting process if they came near the furnace. The belief that women were pollutants to the smelting process arose from the fact that Abagusii viewed iron smelting as a form of procreation. Something raw and cold (ore is the same as semen and ova) could be heated or burnt in the womb (furnace) and then it is transformed into something hot and new (as same as a child). Indeed, the Abagusii referred to the furnace as female and the bellows as male. Women were not allowed to touch the bellows nor pump air into the furnace. If this were done, it could have meant that the woman would be sleeping with the furnace, hence homosexuality, and hence nothing could come out of that union (that is, no iron could be produced).

At the ground level, the furnace had a couple of holes in which tuyeres were inserted. The tuyeres were made of clay while on the other hand, the bellow was made of wood with an open top covered by a goat's skin.

After the construction of the furnace and the insertion of the tuyeres, a fire was lit inside the furnace using *triumfetta* logs. This process of preheating the furnace was necessary as it enabled the tuyeres to be cleaned and thus be able to push the air into the furnace. The pre-heating process was responsible for the rising temperature of the ambient air inside the tuyeres once smelting started, and this led to the attainment of high temperatures inside the furnace itself. The result of this process was the production of high-carbon steel rather than a bloom (Kiriama 1986, 1987). After being satisfied that the tuyeres had cleaned enough, the smelter could then start the actual smelting. He did this by putting charcoal (gotten from acacia tree) and the ore in alternate thin layers such that at the end there was a charcoal layer at the bottom and at the top. The smelter could then light the top layer and from then onwards, quantities of charcoal could be added to make the fire burn more strongly. At each end of the bellows (*emeguba*) men were busy pressing the skin up and down so that air was supplied to the furnace.

The smelting process took about 24 hours to complete. After removing the bloom, the smelter took it to the blacksmith who would manufacture tools such as jembes, pangas, spears and arrowheads, ankle rings (*ebitinge*) for married women and hand rings (*emeotoro*) for old men. Most of these items were, however, made on request.

Smelting was usually done in advance of the digging season to meet the demand during the field clearing and planting season (which was usually from December to January).

While smelters were highly respected and some were fairly rich, they never attained any judicial or political power. This may be due to the fact the smelters never formed a specific guild of their own. Apart from the few taboos associated with it, smelting was not a secret and a smelter could marry anywhere and their daughters could also be married anywhere (with the bridegroom being taught the art of smelting by the father-in-law). This widened the scope of smelting as well as increased the number of smelters and thus helped to prevent only a small group from dominating the rest of society.

Chapter Four

'Ritongo' and 'Omotembe': Abagusii Justice System

The Law and Abagusii

The law can be defined as the enterprise of subjecting human conduct to the governance of rules to enable members of that society to realize a good life as recognized by that society (Kiangoi 1977:3). To enjoy life, a community establishes a justice system that on behalf of the community interprets, defends, and applies the <u>law</u> and also resolves disputes amongst community members. The function of the judicial system therefore is to apply the law. When someone stands accused of a crime, the court supervises a trial, making sure the trial is fair and reasonable. If the person is found guilty, the court can hand down a sentence appropriate to the crime

The Gusii indigenous administration of justice was aimed at solving disputes between parties. Therefore, in the process of dispute resolution the whole social setting and relationships were taken into consideration.

Traditionally, Abagusii society was based on the lineage system called clans. The clan, *egesaku*, was the main unit of Abagusii's social organization. Clan people or *abaamate* were close blood relations who did not intermarry, and each member had a mutual obligation to each other. Therefore, there were rules and regulations that everybody in the community had to adhere to. Transgressions of these rules had legal consequences. To maintain good relations within the clan, people were organized into *etureti* (pl. *chitureti*). The *etureti* was led by elders who were the custodians of customary law and, therefore, were responsible for the settlement of legal disputes.

Abagusii people cherished harmony and peaceful co-existence with others. It was an abomination to kill, let alone spill blood.

It was also taboo for a child to have a bitter exchange with his parents, more so stepfathers and stepmothers. Community life was rooted in *chinsoni* (a clear customized "testament" of does and don'ts for each member of the society). There were serious sanctions and repercussions when one went against the dictates of the community. Killing or critically injuring a member of the community be it at will or by accident was bad news and it was extremely rare. When it happened, people were urged not to revenge. Although it attracted a curse, one would escape this path by seeking forgiveness and offering a special sacrifice to appease God, *Engoro,* and ancestral spirits.

Amongst the Abagusii, dispute resolution was at the core of community survival. Unlike the modern judicial system where the winner takes it all, the Gusii indigenous dispute resolution mechanism entailed arbitration. The advantage of arbitration is that at the end of the process, there is no winner or loser. In other words, arbitration was meant to heal the differences and not sever existing relationships. As a result, the penalty metered to the offender was within manageable limits. This was unlike the modern legal process where the penalty is meant to seek retribution and punishment and not reform. It should also be noted that, unlike today, there were no prisons in Gusii, although extreme offenders could get ostracized from the rest of the community.

The Gusii justice system depended on the trustworthiness of all people involved in the dispute. Occasionally however, craft people would emerge; to mitigate against this a system of oathing was instituted to ensure that whoever appeared before the elders as a complainant, defendant or witness said the truth. Unlike modern days when people swear by the Bible, Koran, or any other religious device, the Abagusii people used *omotembe*[1] (red oak poker tree) to administer oaths. Omotembe is a tree that grows in many parts of Gusii. It has a thick, thorny bark and its canopy provides a good shed. It is said that once somebody made allegations against someone and the defendant denied the allegations, both parties were required to take an oath to determine the veracity of the allegations and denials.

This was done by both parties walking to the Omotembe (which was essentially close to the indigenous court area),

---

1   Editor's Note: Omotembe has similar ritual signifance among the Maragoli of Western Kenya, perhaps underlining the common roots of these two ethnic groups.

stripping naked, holding the tree, and invoking words to the effect that they die if they lied to the elders. This was a very emotive and heart-wrenching step. As one stepped forward, the elders followed and ensured that he/she invoked the words as required. The oath-taking was a do-or-die issue for whoever decided to invoke the oath. Siro Nyaikondo, an elderly man in Ogembo Town, narrated an incident where thunder struck a man dead after he swore before Omotembe that he was innocent and had not hidden anything from the elders. According to Nyaikondo in certain instances, the curse for a person who lied under oath transcended generations.

It should be appreciated that *omotembe* had many other uses. For instance, it was used to make traditional instruments like *obokano* (an 8-stringed lyre) synonymous with the tradition of the Gusii people. It was also used to make domestic receptacles like mortars. It also featured in Gusii ceremonies like circumcision and healing of lymph nodes. Much later, young people used barks of *omotembe* to make rubber stamps. It should however be noted that members of the Gusii community do not convert *Omotembe* to firewood. This is regarded as an abomination that may attract a curse and other forms of suffering to whoever does it. As a result of this, the *omotembe* tree was known as *omonyamuma* (one for taking oaths). Other than oathing, *omotembe* was also said to assist in healing tonsillitis. It is said that when one was diagnosed with tonsillitis, they could gather dry sticks, tie them together and throw the sticks at the tree while uttering the words, "*omotembe onsago (nsago) nchiao echio*" (*omotembe* there is your tonsilitis). It is said that people got healed after performing this ritual.

Apart from *omotembe*, members of the Abagusii community used *orosiaga* (wild nappier grass) for oathing. Unlike what farmers grow to feed their animals, this particular species grew on riverbanks. It was normally used in instances where a man or woman was accused of infidelity. To solve the issue, the accused was supposed to step forward and publicly swear that they were innocent. The man was required to carry a sharpened piece of *orosiaga* and a shield. At the same time, the woman was required to stand some distance ahead, her legs spread apart. Then, the man was expected to go through the legs while saying, "*Onye nakorete aya tiga inkwe* (May I die if I committed this act of shame)". Surprisingly, some died. In modern days, such species of grass are hard to find and are no longer associated with this old-time belief.

As already mentioned, arbitration was at the core of the Gusii community. It was believed that blood brothers should not become adversaries forever. One who did not cede room for reconciliation was a potential candidate for getting ostracized. Those engaged in reconciliation were however expected to uphold honesty and avoid hiding dangerous cards under the table to defeat justice.

During the colonial period, the colonialists converted some of the places of the traditional courts into traditional colonial courts (Native Courts) which locals called *Ritongo*. Some of these places include Manga and Gesima in Nyamira County and Ogembo and Ritumbe in Kisii County. During our research, we found out that *omotembe* was used at least in one of these native courts especially in Manga for oathing purposes though it had been cut down a while ago. According to our informants, the tree was cut down during the construction of the juvenile remand home that now occupies the area of the former Ritongo.

Currently, the Gesima and Ogembo courts serve as government offices while some of the buildings in Manga have been converted into a juvenile remand centre while others have been renovated to serve as formal courts. Also, currently, there is a magistrate court at Ogembo. Ritumbe, other than being a gazetted forest with exotic plants also has offices of the local chief.

Ritongo was particularly adjudicated by the elders. It was believed that as one advanced in age, he became wiser and could make better decisions. Therefore, those who met the criteria to sit in *Ritongo* had to be people of great repute and integrity. Such people were expected to be above reproach. They had to be individuals who would not accept bribes or favour any party during the arbitration/ case hearing process. They were also expected to be patient and a good listener who would take time to let others talk, and, people who would consult before arriving at a decision that would be binding. Issues that found their way to Ritongo included land disputes, theft, and infidelity.

A stream that is very encroached with exotic vegetation particularly eucalyptus in Nyamira County.

Men at Entono in Bonchari Constituency. The area has a special "well" whose water is associated with blessings and protection of families and individuals.

One of the few ritualistic trees remaining in Gusii region.

This tree (omotembe) was significant in oathing amongst Abagusii.

The Water Flour Mills.

One of the greatest complexes of life is telling, what, between the egg and the hen came first. This may not be the same case when one looks at grains and flour. One can be sure that grains came first for one can only get flour out of the grains.

Before maize was introduced in Kenya probably by the Portuguese in the 16th century and eventually became the staple food of many Kenyan communities, Abagusii and other indigenous Kenyan communities depended on other types of food for survival. These foods included meat from both domestic and wild animals, fruits, and grains like finger millet. Most of these crops were eaten raw or after boiling and roasting. As for finger millet, *wimbi*, the indigenous communities such as the Gusii used grinding stones *(ensio)* to manually convert the grains to flour. They would then cook porridge or ugali. The grinding process was time-consuming, and the output was relatively low. The people had to contend with the method since they did not have an alternative. It should be borne in mind that at this time, before colonialism, there were no petrol/diesel-powered or electric mills. These were introduced much later.

Other than manual grinding of the grains, some people used water mills to do the grinding. It should however be noted that the history of water mills is quite old. The first documented use of water mills was made in England, in the first Century Before the Common Era (BCE), and the technology spread quite quickly across the world. By the 16th Century of the Common Era (CE or AD), waterpower was the most important source of locomotive power in Britain and Europe. Water mills continued to play an important role in British rural life and were in growing demand, as improvements in farming techniques enabled farmers to produce even more maize and other forms of cereals that were being grounded in water mills to make flour.

But how does a water mill work? A water mill uses moving water as its power source to drive a mechanical process such as milling, grinding, rolling or hammering. Water mills use the flow of water to turn a large waterwheel. A shaft connected to the wheel axle is then used to transmit the power from the water through a system of gears and cogs to the work machinery, such as a millstone to grind grains such as millet or maize. The water mills were located along river courses and especially along fast-flowing rivers or rivers with waterfalls because the mill requires a steep gradient on the channel so that the velocity is enhanced. The force of the water's movement drives the blades of a turbine, which in turn rotates an axle that drives the mill's other parts. Water leaving the turbine is drained through an exit at the tail, but it can still be used as a head race of yet another wheel, turbine, or mill. The water is controlled by sluice gates. This provides room for maintenance when there is a need. It is also a measure of flood control.

Most common water mills are constructed in a horizontal position in which the force of the water, striking a simple paddle wheel set horizontally in line with the flow turned a runner stone balanced on the rynd. The rynd was placed atop a shaft leading directly up from the wheel. There was a static bedstone which ensured that the grains dropped on it were ground into fine flour by the rotating stone placed on top of the static bedstone. The main undoing of this technology is that it lacked a gearing system. Thus, the speed of the water directly determined the maximum speed of the runner stone which, in turn, set the rate of milling.

This innovation, powered by fast-flowing water channelled from a canal or stream to turn the heavy grindstone to produce flour fed hundreds of people in the past. With the availability of many rivers in Gusii, it was not difficult for enterprising individuals to embrace the technology. The advent of the water mills triggered people to start looking for huge stones that would be used to make them. However, such stones were a rarity across Gusiiland.

However, the stones were known to be readily available in Bonchari. Therefore, the first water mill was established along River Riana in Bonchari since the river was not far from the source of the stones. Zebedeo, Omwega and Keng'otore who were brothers were among the early investors in this enterprise. As word spread, more people came in for the stones which they transported to their homes and used to establish power mills of their own. Such mills were established along River Gucha, Echarachani, Nyamotentemi, Bonyunyu, Eyaka, Nyameru, and Nyabomite, among others. Around Ogembo Town, three brothers;

Abner Arori, Absolom Ondara and Paul Machuki equally ventured into the enterprise, relying on water diverted from River Gucha.

It is not known when watermills were introduced into Kenya and Gusiiland and by whom. From anecdotal evidence, we can only say that this technology may have been introduced sometime in the mid-20th century. There are, however, arguments, without much evidence, that watermills may have been introduced into Gusii by Indian traders sometime in the 20th century. For instance, an interviewee by the name of Henry Oroti recalls that he saw a water mill for the first time in 1950. At that time, he was a young boy. The mill belonged to Mzee Orengo who charged as little as 2 cents to grind two kilogrammes of grains. Oroti further stated that what he noticed was that it had a handle that was used to adjust the speed at which the propeller and the grinding stones turned. When the stone turned slowly, the flour became finer than when the stone turned faster.

It can be argued that water-powered mills became popular in Gusii between 1945 and the early 1980s. For instance, Mzee Makori Ondieki's mill was established in 1945 at Charachani River in Nyamira. Ondieki says he inherited it from his grandfather and has operated it since that time. His is among the few if not the only mill that is in good condition to this day, although he rarely operates it. Informants told us that along the Charachani River, there was another mill which was popular with local residents. The mill belonged to a man known as Nyamanga. Local folk history has it that a girl, by the name of Nyaboke Monyoncho, was sent by her mother to the posho mill. On her way back, Nyaboke, who was carrying a baby on her back, met with a "woman" who requested Nyaboke to give her some flour. Nyaboke is said to have flatly refused. Suddenly, there was rummaging and in the commotion, the river shook violently and swelled. In a twinkle of an eye, the mysterious woman disappeared just as she had appeared. This was followed by a sudden flood that swept Nyaboke downstream. The angry flood uprooted trees, and the water mill and killed several animals. It was expected that Nyaboke's body would be found once the flood subsided but this never came to pass. Nyaboke's body was never found! Following the tragic news, a song was composed in memory of Nyaboke's disappearance from the face of the earth. The song went like this:

(Echarachani eee ekaira Nyaboke)x2	*(River Charachani swept Nyaboke)*
Baito! Echarani eee ekaira Nyaboke!	*(People! Charachani swept Nyaboke)*
Menamenia amareko torore e'simba....	*(Shake your shoulders...)*

It should be appreciated that long queues were often witnessed at the water mills. This was because they were relatively slow. The introduction of maize also boosted the demand for maize flour that could only be obtained from these mills. This was unlike finger millet that could be ground at home. Once people took their grains to the mills, they could wait for up to three days before their grains were ground. This meant that one had to be clever and take his grains to the mills in advance, that is, before exhausting flour at home. Without doing this, a family stood a chance of going, without their meal for a day or two.

As years progressed, posho mills powered by diesel were introduced. These relatively faster machines did not need to be placed near rivers. Although they charged relatively higher fees compared to water mills, people quickly embraced them. The fact that they were situated closer to human settlements unlike water mills gave them a head start in weakening water mills. With time, owners of water mills closed shop. Many of these ancient mills have been destroyed and cannot be traced.

It is unfortunate that although the rivers are intact, albeit with lower volumes of water that have also been contaminated due to human activities, most water mills have been phased out. Worse yet, the know-how of starting and operating one has disappeared with the demise of the previous generations. The tragedy of this story is compounded by the fact that when one visits the sites where these water mills were situated; one can hardly find any trace or evidence of their existence. It is therefore important and urgent that the one operated by Makori at Charachani River be jealously protected and preserved for posterity.

Also, during our field research in the Nyabieyo area of Bonchari, our assistant, Evans Oriri, led us to a piece of land occupied with blue gum trees, just a few metres from the Riana River. The trees were surrounded by sugarcane and bamboo. In the middle of the trees, we traced a round stone. Its diameter was around one metre. In the middle, it had a hole and according to Oriri, this may have been the runner stone of one of the water mills in the area.

The technology of turning grains into flour continues to advance. The use of stones to manually grind finger millet is currently almost extinct, and so is the use of water mills. Equally, mills powered by diesel are facing competition from electric mills. The electric mills are considerably faster and use clean energy. This gives them an advantage over those powered by diesel.

Chapter Five

Other Sacred Places

Entono Herbal Area

Next to Entono SDA Church in Bonchari Constituency is a rocky patch that is covered with indigenous vegetation. The vegetation includes herbaceous and medicinal plants such as *emekubo, emeraa, emetaburo, emetaraganga,* among others. Most of these herbs blossomed in many places within Gusii and they were used by traditional herbalists before the advent of modern medicine to treat various ailments. With the exponential growth of the population, such herbs are hard to find since they have been uprooted to pave the way for food production. For this reason, herbalists come from far and wide to look for herbs at Entono.

There is more to Entono other than the herbs. It is what gives the place the name, *Entono* (symbolic of a small traditional pot used to carry or store water for domestic use). Within the bush, there is an "underground pot" that never gets filled with water. It is not a pot but a depression whose diameter is 40 cm. What remains unknown is its depth since when one inserts a stick into it, it does not go more than 60 cm deep.

What baffles members of the community and visitors alike is the fact that the "pot" seems almost full of water all the time yet it never overflows. Interestingly again, once one fetches the water, the volume that reduces is equivalent to the water scooped but not for long; the water rises again to its usual level before one even leaves. Two similar holes which are relatively smaller in size and also have little water each, and not enough for one to scoop, are also situated in the Entono area.

The story of Entono is difficult to comprehend even after one listens to the locals, they too do not understand the mysterious phenomenon in their midst. To them, they believe that this piece of land is a historical ground, and it probably sits on an underground lake. Interviewees Evans Nyayio and Francis Orang'i who are both aged over 60 years say the water in these three holes has been there over the years, come rain or sunshine.

But they insist it is not just any other water; it is sacred and therefore it should be approached circumspectly. Therefore, as with other sacred heritage sites within Gusii, there is a clear procedure that one must follow whenever he visits Entono. This starts with uprooting and tying up green grass some 50 metres away from the "holy" ground. One then carries the grass to the hole where he drops it beside the "pot." Secondly, when one gets to the "holes" one must drop a coin (Sh5, 10 or 20) into the water, failure to which the water will disappear until the person leaves. Interestingly, neither the grass nor the coins have filled or blocked nor interfered with the level the water rises to. No one can tell where the coins disappear but it is generally agreed by the locals that the grass eventually dries up and is collected by herbalists who use it to treat several health-related complications.

As already indicated, according to our interviewees, Entono is a sacred place. They believe that in the past, mysterious people, perhaps spirits, resided at the place. We were told that in the past, one could hear strange human voices engrossed in song and dance amidst the enticing sounds of *Obokano* (a Gusii traditional eight-stringed musical instrument). Strangely, the voices went silent as one got closer to the "sacred place." In reality, nobody ever saw the "singers" as much as everyone agreed that those were human voices.

Over time, people have continued to visit *Entono*. Some visit the place to collect herbs while others come to the place for adventure. Still others visit the place just to fetch the sacred water. And they have strong convictions that the water from *entono* is not just any other water. They believe that water has some supernatural powers that include healing and protecting one from evil and misfortune.

Thus, it should be stated that as much as a majority of Abagusii people have abandoned ancient practices that they consider backward, a majority of those who visit Entono insist that the water can cure evil. Some sprinkle the water in their compounds believing that it can deter intruders from harming. To some, the water can deter evil people including witches from harming them. This belief is held close by the residents to the extent that they fail to understand why one would visit *entono* with only a small container to carry the water.

Importantly again, in the past, the ground was used to perform a traditional rain dance, locally known as *Ribina*. This was a special dance performed to plead to God to return rain after a prolonged drought. While women danced, young men held a wrestling match nearby. The community believed that the song, dance, and wrestling would bring rain. The story of *ribina* is covered comprehensively in another section of this book.

However, it should be appreciated that *ribina* attracted people from far and wide. The women religiously performed the dance and indeed, at times, thick clouds gathered while the performance was underway and the heavens opened for a heavy downpour soon after. If it did not fall that same day, then it did a day or two later.

This traditional performance was perhaps an indicator that since time immemorial, mankind communicated with God who is the giver of rain, life and blessings of all kinds. Entono SDA church sits on a plot donated by Evans Nyayio. The church building is a stone's throw away from the mysterious holes. To Nyayio, bringing the SDA church to his area was meant to reinforce the fact that they appreciate God's supernatural and omniscient works.

Although the land is reserved as government property, there is a possibility of it being put into maximum use at any time in the near future due to the rapid increase in human population. The ground is not fenced up and is potential fodder for land grabbers. In the meantime, local people act as tour guides. They gladly welcome strangers and take them around, telling them the unique story behind this area. They look forward to the day scientists will undertake a study and help them understand the archaeological and scientific logic behind this unique heritage site.

Omosasa Sacred Tree

On the upper side of the Manga Escarpment, the late celebrated Senior Chief Zachary Angwenyi's land terminates at the Manga cliff. There is a path that adjoins Angwenyi's land from the lower side of the cliff. This is one of the few paths that link the lower and upper parts of Manga. It is locally called *Egesieri* (door).

For many years, there stood a special tree *(omosasa o'Kegancha)* beside the path. The tree, believed to have fallen on its own a few years ago had been in existence for several decades. Wherever *Omosasa* tree grew anywhere in Gusii, it was never allowed to be cut, be it for firewood or timber. Interestingly, such ritualistic trees were relatively few. Apart from *Omosasa o'Kegancha,* there was another at Nyambaria Geke near Nyambaria High School.

Oral tradition has it that some men who attempted to cut the *Omosasa* tree at the Manga Escarpment got themselves in trouble. One reportedly got injured when the axe he was using flew in the air and fell on his leg while another became mentally unstable. Omosasa o'Kegancha eventually came down after rotting from the inside. Its stability was also compromised by many years of erosion. Even so, members of the local community did not collect it for firewood nor convert it to timber. Eventually, a non-local person cut the fallen tree into small pieces and carted them away.

According to the local people, Omosasa o'Kegancha was very significant to their ancestors. They say that it was their ancestors' hideout during attacks by raiders particularly from the Kalenjin community. It also possessed some supernatural powers that protected the community from harm. As a result, thieves, including cattle raiders got captured easily whenever they used the path next to the tree.

As already stated, Abagusii believed that curses *(ebiranya)* worked in favour of the community. They therefore hid their ritualistic paraphernalia at the tree and invoked curses or sought forgiveness from their ancestors by performing special prayers and sacrifices there. It is believed that such sacrifices and prayers attracted barren women who, eventually got blessed with children.

Lake Okari

At the foot of the rocky belt of Manga Escarpment sits Getebo village and within the area is Lake Okari. This is the only lake in Gusii but it has shrunk in size over time. The volume of water at present does not give any hint that it is possibly a lake. One may call it a dam.

According to geologists, Lake Okari is one of three natural sponges in southwestern Kenya that feeds rivers, springs and boreholes in the region. Furthermore, Lakes Okari, Victoria and Simbi Nyaima in Homa Bay County are the only lakes of their kind in Kenya and may have been formed millions of years ago. Lake Okari itself measures about 50 by 70 metres and was formed in 1965 through a process where rocks bend and sink due to exerted tectonic pressure to create a water reservoir. However, the lake has been diminishing in size in recent years as a result of geological changes that caused a crack in this area and other parts of Western Kenya. This geological phenomenon of massive tectonic movements eventually formed elongated rifts from the Red Sea to Mozambique and will make the Sea water from the Indian Ocean connect with Lake Victoria and other lakes in the Great Rift Valley region.

Local history indicates that Lake Okari occupies land that was once owned by a man called Okari. It is further stated that the lake was formed after part of Okari's land which was initially flat caved in. Due to the resultant danger, Okari and his family members were moved to the Borabu settlement scheme where they were allocated land to settle. Hence, this lake was named after the original owner of the land.

In its early days, the lake had several fish, particularly tilapia species. Villagers believed that Lake Okari and Lake Victoria were interlinked with an underground canal. As a result, fish came in from Lake Victoria and as much as they fished them, they never got depleted. They also believed that Lake Okari drained its waters into Lake Victoria through the underground canal since it never got full nor overflowed.

Presently, the lake does not look like one. It is covered with reeds and other vegetation. There are several gum trees and food crops around it too. It is believed that human activities such as the planting of eucalyptus, coffee, and maize, doubled with siltation have contributed to the lake's diminishing in size.

In particular, Lake Okari is situated in a village which is densely populated and the people need land for cultivation. As a result, people have encroached on areas adjacent to the lake and the more this happens, the smaller it becomes. Geologists hint that geological activities that have hit the area in the recent past are an indication that the underlying rocks and underground activities are similar to those found around active volcanic areas. This portends possible danger to the people in some years to come.

For instance, in 2019, there was panic when local people reported that huge cracks had formed near the lake. Authorities at the time said that they were assessing the escarpment amidst fears that a landslide would occur and cause massive damage to property and loss of life. The cracks had affected several floors of residents' houses.

The news occasioned an emergency response by a multi-agency team that came in to study the rare phenomenon. The then Kisii County Commissioner, Stephen Kihara, said that there were fears that the worst could happen since geologists had confirmed that indeed there was a lot of underground water there. At the time, several families were moved to nearby schools for temporary shelter. They eventually returned when the rains subsided.

Moreover, the adjacent Marani area is prone to landslides. In 2020, residents of Riabotenene and Nyabworoba had to flee their homes after their land started to sink due to landslides following a heavy downpour. Over 150 people were affected. During this period, fault lines were formed starting from the Manga Escarpment to the two villages. Furthermore, the nearby Nyamokamba stream suddenly grew into a river, posing questions if the area was safe for human settlement.

This notwithstanding, a handful of local people and students continue visiting Lake Okari for learning purposes. Having conservation thoughts in mind, they argue that the lake should be protected from human activities that endanger its survival.

From the foregoing, it can be argued that there is a need for the whole of the Manga Escarpment and the adjacent areas to be protected. Protection will include fencing up the area and ensuring that people exploiting the resource for personal gain, particularly in terms of cultivation and quarrying are properly managed if not stopped altogether.

The area can also be used as a picnicking, sightseeing and refresher natural trail area. This, alongside the establishment of hotels, a good road network, and a museum to preserve existing Gusii artifacts may go a long way in safeguarding the rich history of the Manga Escarpment and the entire Gusii community.

There have been promises from the County Governments of Kisii and Nyamira of rehabilitating the place due to its rich history, fascinating sceneries, and heritage sites but all this has not translated into action.

The Unique Stone: Rigena Ria Kwamboka

This is found in the Bonchari area. The huge rock lies on top of a smaller rock, and it swings when pushed. However, the rock cannot fall even when pushed hard. The rock served as a communication centre when there was a need to alert the community of an occurrence. Circumcision rituals were also conducted here.

Existing Unique Waterfalls

A waterfall is an area where river water drops abruptly and falls nearly vertically and there are big interruptions in river flow. Waterfalls that have a small height and lesser steepness are called cascades. Waterfalls are formed when streams flow from soft rock to hard rock. This happens as a stream flows across the earth's surface (laterally) and as it drops in a waterfall (moves vertically). In both cases, the soft rock erodes, leaving a hard ledge over which the stream falls; meaning therefore that erosion plays a major role in the formation of waterfalls. As a stream flows, it carries sediments.

The sediments can be very small silt, pebbles, or even boulders. Sediments erode stream beds made of soft rock, such as sandstone or limestone. Eventually, the stream's channel cuts so deep into the stream bed that only a harder rock, such as granite, remains. Waterfalls develop as these granite formations form cliffs and ridges. A stream's speed increases as it nears a waterfall, increasing the amount of erosion taking place. The movement of water at the top of a waterfall can erode rocks making them flat and smooth. Rushing water and sediments topple over the waterfall, eroding the bottom plunge of the pool at the base. The crashing flow of the water may also create powerful whirlpools that erode the rock of the plunge pool beneath them.

In many cultures, a waterfall is often used to symbolize the flow of life. Water from rivers flows through so many different terrains before entering the ocean. A waterfall completes the flow of the river in the formation of its life cycle. It may also symbolize the flow of a human being's life cycle. It is therefore used in many societies as a symbol to show the fact that human life has a flow, path, and rhythm of life in which it has got to pass through.

Nyameru Waterfall (Ekeera)

About four kilometres from Nyamira Town is the Rangenyo area. The area is home to Rangenyo Girls School, Rangenyo Primary School, and Rangenyo Catholic Parish, among other academic, religious, and social installations. Not far from Rangenyo, one finds the largest waterfall *(ekeera)* in the whole of Nyamira County.

The waterfall would not be in existence without the presence of the Nyabomite River, whose source is the Tente[1] wetland. The swamp starts from the lower side of the current Nyamira police station and extends to the Tente area. It is from here that the water oozes from the ground and then moves lazily down to Rangenyo where the gradient falls sharply, necessitating the formation of the waterfall at Nyambati Ituka's land as the water cascades its course.

At the foot of the waterfall is a cave that has been in existence for many years. As is the case with such heritage sites, it is said that in the past, local people believed that a mysterious man, Nyamoerere, lived in the cave. It is believed that Nyamoerere possessed supernatural powers and did not welcome and/or interact with strangers. However, whoever wanted to visit the cave had to carry a bundle of firewood for Nyamoerere. Once one got there, he threw the firewood into the cave believing that Nyamoerere would use it to light a fire in the evening to warm himself. This belief stayed in the people's minds because each time they visited the cave, they only found ash and assumed that Nyamoerere had used the firewood that was left behind for him.

Thus, in the past, local people believed that the cave was an abode for their ancestral spirits. Consequently, whenever anyone was confronted with any challenge or misfortune, they went to the caves to pray and offer sacrifices to the ancestors. They believed that the spirits could be appeased to protect them from such misfortunes.

---

1   Editor's Note: *etente* means wetland and *tente* refers to the place where there is *etente*. However, note that etente is a different form of wetland from *ekerubo*, the latter, also a wetland, would be some flat field that turns soggy when it rains.

Following the discovery of water-powered mills in the 1950s, two locals, James Nyambati and Mokobo Agai partnered and established a water mill at Ekeera. The mill served many people, some from as far as Egesieri, Etono, Rangenyo, Nyamaiya and Metobo. However, the water mill eventually collapsed. Presently, there is nothing that indicates that once upon a time there was a water mill there.

For many years also, the cave was home to a swam of bees. Nobody claimed ownership of the bees which produced a lot of honey from time to time. The honey was harvested by young men and consumed at the field or taken to be shared with their family members. It is not clear when the bees eventually left.

As indicated, there is a Catholic Parish at Rangenyo, a stone-throw away from the waterfall. History has it that in the late 1940s, an elder by the name of Kiriago who hailed from Gekendo in North Mugirango Constituency served as an interpreter at the colonial court in Kisii. Kiriago was among the very few men from the area who had been introduced to formal education. This gave him an edge when he interacted with white missionaries who had established a Catholic Church at Nyabururu on the outskirts of Kisii.

Following these interactions, Kiriago admired the Christian way of life and thought it wise to introduce it to his people back at Gekendo. He therefore requested the church leadership and it was honored. However, when the missionaries built a semi-permanent church at Gekendo, the local people were not amused. To register their protest, they set the grass-thatched church on fire at night.

At this time, there was no ready vehicular transport in the area and the road network was poor. To reach Gekendo from Nyabururu, the missionaries had to pass through Rangenyo, and they admired the place. They liked the raised topography of Rangenyo, as one could see most parts of Gusii and beyond from there. They were therefore contemplating that Rangenyo would be more strategic for new converts if they erected a church there. They also managed to befriend a successful elder by the name Nyairo from Bonyaiguba who in turn influenced them that Rangenyo would be ideal for the church project. That humble beginning eventually culminated in the present parish, schools, health Centre, and other amenities critical to people's lives.

It is important to note that the stories of the Catholic Church at Rangenyo and that of the waterfall cannot be delinked. This is particularly so because once the missionaries discovered the waterfall, they started frequenting it for prayers. This went on for many years. Perhaps the deteriorating state of the paths leading to the place because of encroachment by the local people is to blame for the eventual withdrawal of the Christians' visits to the site.

Away from the already listed unique attributes of the waterfall, it is crucial to observe that indigenous trees which surrounded it acted as the habitat of various species of birds. However, the scenic beauty has been destroyed over time. Presently, the waterfall is surrounded by mainly eucalyptus trees and very few birds. Local people have also cultivated the land around it and this complicates access as it borders on trespassing on people's agricultural land.

For years yonder, Nyabomite River provided clean water for domestic use. Cattle also quenched their thirst there. This is no longer the case now. The river has drastically shrunk. It now looks like a disappearing stream. Its volumes only rise during the rainy season when flashflood water finds its way into the river. The rainwater equally sweeps waste and harmful chemicals like fertilizers from agricultural farms into the river. This worsens the water's safety for drinking either by cattle or humans.

It is also important to note that in recent years, Nyamira Town has recorded exponential population growth. This scenario has been fueled by the devolved administrative system that has established counties such as Nyamira. Many people have purchased pieces of land in the town and its environs and have built homes. There are also more schools, colleges, churches, and health facilities in the area.

Downstream, the Nyabomite River joins the Motobo River at Bonyunyu before it proceeds to be swallowed by the Echarachani River in Kisii County. The river becomes part of Osaosao River not far from the Kisii-Homa Bay border and eventually finds its way into Lake Victoria.

Perhaps conservation efforts should be made to save the river, and ensure it provides safe, abundant, and clean water for the people and their livestock. Such efforts will also restore the surrounding riparian water ecosystem. The river used to be a source of fish and home to water beetles, whose presence signalled that it was not contaminated. Removal of eucalyptus from along the river banks and particularly the waterfall will also restore its lost glory. The waterfall can also be used to tap electricity and attract tourists.

A shot of Ekeera waterfall found in Rangenyo area of Nyamira County.

Chapter Six

Historical Figures and Indigenous Rain Dance

As physical and intangible landscapes are important heritage places, we also consider human beings, those players/actors in these landscapes, as part of the indigenous heritage. It is the actions or pronouncements of these individuals that affirm or destroy the importance of these landscapes; the actions of such individuals give significance to the heritage landscapes. It is against this backdrop that we include a few of the historical figures of Gusiiland in this book.

Sakagwa Ng'iti

Sakagwa (Sakawa) is considered the most important Gusii prophet of the 19th Century. It is said that after the death of Mogusii, the eponymous founder of the Abagusii, the community started to split into different groups, such as Abagetutu, Abagirango and Abanyaribari. These groups had individuals who gave rise to their families such as Bogonko who gave rise to Mwabogonko, and Manwa gave rise to Mwamanwa) Bundusi gave rise to Mwabundusi and so on. From Mwabundusi came Ogeka who gave rise to the Bogeka family.

In the Bogeka family, around the late eighteenth century and early in the nineteenth century, a man known as Nyakembugumbugu was born. Later on, Nyakembugumbugu became the father of a son known as Ng'iti who, with his wife Nyabosungire were the parents of Sakagwa. Ngiti on his own was also a famous magician and rainmaker. Though Ng'iti had many wives, he, however, only begot daughters, and Sakawa was his only son. As an only son, Sakawa inherited from his father the art of rainmaking and the use of indigenous herbs.

According to oral history, Sakagwa was fond of telling people short stories that foretold the future. He could also pronounce curses on people and these curses came to pass. Though this created a hate/love relationship between him and other members of the community, people recognized him as a great prophet, a warrior, a medicine man, a rainmaker, a community sage and a family person. His prophesies were taken seriously because they always came to pass. Sakagwa, for instance, prophesied that Kisii Town, then known as Getembe, would someday become a major business and economic hub. In his prophesy he said, *"amandegere name getembe ore na bamura nere orayae* (mushrooms will sprout in Getembe and he who has sons will harvest them). By this, he meant that not everyone would get a share of the town but he whose sons were keen to take up the opportunity as it arose.

Sakagwa may have been born in the mid-nineteenth century at Getwanyansi in present-day Kitutu Chache. In his youth, Sakagwa became one of the community warriors as there were several skirmishes with other neighbouring communities, especially the Kipsigis and the Maasai at that time. This made Sakagwa move to North Mugirango which was the epicentre of the conflicts between the Abagusii and the Kipsigis. During these wars, Sakagwa is said to have assisted the Abagusii war efforts by applying some magic, commonly known as *ebiranya,* that is said to have confused the enemies and led to Abagusii's victory over them. These made Abagusii warriors heavily rely on Sakagwa's word. He could warn them of lurking danger. He equally foresaw their triumph in upcoming confrontations with their adversaries. For instance, before the Osaosao/Mogori skirmishes where Kipsigis warriors were killed to a man, Sakagwa had given his community warriors blessings that this was their turn to triumph for the good of the Gusii people.

Over time, Sakagwa became very influential and yet he remained to be a mysterious being. People never understood him and the source of his mysterious powers. Equally, Sakagwa made enemies of his own, particularly from ethnic communities that neighboured the Gusii people. Towards the end, controversy surrounded Sakagwa's life and mysterious death and burial in 1902.

A. Sakagwa's Grave

Although there is no tombstone or any physical mark, it is believed that Sakagwa's grave is separated by a fence with Sakagwa Primary School in Gesoni village, Kitutu Chache constituency; the family of Sakagwa knows where he was buried. The school, which started as a nursery school unit, was established in 2007. It is now a fully registered primary school with over 600 pupils. The institution stands on the sage's land ostensibly to perpetuate his name many years after his mysterious death. Its establishment also reduced pressure on St Peter's Soko Primary School whose facilities had been overstretched following a notably bigger influx of learners following the introduction of free primary school education by President Mwai Kibaki's administration in 2003. Much of Sakagwa's land was regarded as a shrine but this status has been adulterated over time.

Initially, there was a pile of stones around and on top of Sakagwa's grave. Over time, the stones were taken away to be used in the construction of houses. Cultivation has also taken place and it is difficult for one to identify where the grave is without the assistance of the family. Within the school compound, there are two communication masts of two telecommunication companies. The masts were erected there ahead of the school. A water supply tank, a lighting transformer and the existing school give a glimpse of development that ought to be enhanced to place Sakagwa's name where it belongs.

Right outside the school compound, there is a lot of green vegetation on a rocky patch. Much of the vegetation is herbal. Thus, herbalists come to the area from far and wide to collect the herbs which they use to treat various ailments. Remarkable is the fact that the height of nearly all the vegetation and herbal trees is lower than that of *Omoraa o'Sakagwa*. This is a particular tree under which Sakagwa spent most of his time. The position offered him a clear view of his land as well as neighbouring and distant villages. This way, he could spot intruders from afar and take caution. The tree is held in special regard by the family and the adjacent community, and it is unimaginable that anybody will ever cut it. Some believe that touching it enhances one's luck in life.

About 3 metres from the tree, there is a spring that never dries up. The spring has been in existence for many years. It is from this spring that Sakagwa drew water for drinking. The water appears to percolate from the rocks and disappear underground soon after.

Overall, it can be said that Sakagwa was one of the greatest members of the Gusii community who ever lived. It can also be noted that Sakagwa made a huge contribution to the survival and success of the community. It is therefore unfortunate that neither his grave nor his shrine is protected. Everything that could give an inkling and trace of the prophet is now facing a threat of extinction. The integration of modern installations like communication masts and the school is a good step in the right direction. Even so, there is a need for the shrine and grave to be protected so that this part of Gusii heritage is not fully whipped from the face of the world.

B. The Famous Gusii Warrior: Otenyo Nyamaterere

Otenyo Nyamaterere[1]

---

1   NB: this picture, obtained from the Internet, may or may not be that of Otenyo the Kisii warrior.

Away from Sakagwa, a renowned Gusii warrior Otenyo Nyamaterere deserves a mention. Otenyo's name entered the annals when he led a contingent of over 500 Gusii warriors who attacked and managed to repulse the British colonial soldiers from the Bonchari and Kitutu areas. The bloody encounter between the Gusii warriors and the British soldiers frightened a section of the community who felt that it had infuriated the British soldiers to decimate them. But to others, the attack was a sign that the community would eventually manage to kick the invader out of their land. But how did the attack begin? In 1904, a group of Abagusii warriors raided a neighbouring Luo community. This raid, however, irked the British colonial government which sent a contingent of over 100 soldiers and 50 policemen to punish the so-called belligerent Abagusii tribesmen. This expedition was led by one, Milton who was a ruthless soldier; the expedition went wild, torching homes and looting. In one incident alone, more than 100 people were moved down with machine gun fire.

Particularly, in Milton's ranks (i.e. the leader of the colonial expedition) was a young political officer called GAS Northcote. Three years after this massacre, Northcote rose the ranks and was sent to Kisii as its first colonial administrator. Later on, the British soldiers under Northcote made numerous invasions on Abagusii cattle camps known as *ebisarate* and seized livestock. One British raid that stands out happened in 1908 when they raided *ebisarate* in the Kitutu region and confiscated over 8,000 livestock. A famous warrior who had survived one of the initial attacks was Otenyo Nyamaterere (a lead warrior from the Kitutu clan) who was angered with the serious losses of livestock and planned a counterattack on the British soldiers who were by then marching livestock out of Kitutu.

With the encouragement of Moraa Ng'iti, a famous medicine woman who is said to have been his aunt, Otenyo assembled a group of over 100 fierce warriors to launch a counterattack. Armed with arrows and spears, they used a different route and got ahead of the British soldiers who were moving slowly with the livestock. Once they were in front of them, the Gusii warriors waylaid the British officers by spreading themselves out and hiding inside a thicket of bushes. Through the ambush, the Gusii warriors managed to repulse the colonial soldiers and recover many livestock which they led towards the Manga Escarpment.

Three days after the attack, the British launched another punitive expedition against Abagusii that led to over 100 people being killed. On their side, over 20 British soldiers were also killed, and; as they were retreating towards Getembe (the administrative headquarters), the colonial administrator, Northcote, who was in charge of the expedition was, almost fatally wounded. He had to spend several months recuperating from the near-fatal attack.

With the eventual conquest of the Gusii, the colonial administration gave a decree for Gusii's lead warrior Otenyo Nyamaterere to surrender to the British as a sign that the Gusii had been subdued. As per the colonialists' conditionality, the Gusii elders convinced Otenyo to give himself for the overall survival of the Gusii community. Indeed, as a patriotic Gusii warrior, Otenyo had to heed the elders' request so that he could save his community from further anguish.

It is important to note that several Gusii elders accompanied Otenyo when he surrendered himself to the colonial administration in the headquarters at Getembe (present-day Kisii Town).

Otenyo Nyamaterere was then executed by a firing squad and his lifeless body was beheaded. Under the guidance of the Gusii elders, Otenyo's headless body was buried at the precincts of Getembe Town and his head was taken to London as proof of his death. It should also be noted that Otenyo's skull remains in a British museum to this day.

In recent years, there have been calls by the Gusii community, led by the Gusii Council of Elders that the head of Otenyo is returned to Kenya to allow for a decent burial.

C. **Moraa Ng'iti**

It is worth noting that, for a long time amongst the Abagusii, women were not supposed to speak before men. Not even when they had an idea that would work well for the good of the Gusii community. Patriarchy was deeply entrenched in the community. It is for this reason that a woman, Moraa Ng'iti, stood out.

Moraa was born in the early years of 1800 in Bogeka, a sub-clan of Bogetutu.. During her time, roles between men and women were clearly defined and crossing the boundaries was an abomination. Men protected families and owned land and family property. Women as well as children were considered to form part of men's property.

In such a scenario, women were there to be seen and not to be heard. It was rather strange that Moraa chose to go against the grain following the invasion of the land by colonialists. Though she hailed from the Bogetutu clan, her resolve made her name spread in the length and breadth of the land of Abagusii.

Moraa is said to have had vast knowledge of indigenous medicine. Just like Sakagwa, Moraa's "prophecies" came to pass. She prophesied that the land would be invaded by Europeans and that men should be ready to take them on. However, she put a caution. That one man from the community would eventually betray them. This came to pass when one, Ombati became a collaborator of the white man. Ombati could steal secrets from his people and disclose them to their enemy. As such, the community suffered at the hands of the colonialists since they could thwart their combat at war easily.

It is said that when 1905 Geoffrey Northcote a British colonial officer, carried out wanton killings of Abagusii people, this irked Moraa and the two became personal enemies to the extent Northcote reportedly said this about the Abagusii, "They are peaceful enough but it is their high priestess that causes me anxious moments. She has been aloof and broods, with anger in her heart and suspicion."

Hostility between the Gusii people and the colonial administration went on unabated. There was a general feeling amongst the indigenous people that the foreigners had to leave their land at whatever cost. What brought things to the fore was the institution of hut tax in 1907 by the colonial authorities and the insistence by the colonialists that the tax had to be paid in cash. This forced many Abagusii to sell their possessions such as cattle, goats, and sheep to get the cash with which they could pay the tax. To Moraa and many other Abagusii, Northcote was the symbol of British colonialism. His removal would have led to an end to the British occupation of Gusiiland.

John S. Akama writes in **The Untold Story: *Gusii Survival Techniques and Resistance to the Establishment of British Colonia Rule,*** that during a community meeting at Manga Hill, all present agreed that the Gusii were confronting a formidable enemy which required a concerted effort from all Gusii clans to protect their motherland. On several occasions, the British under

Northcote made invasions of Abagusii cattle camps. For instance in 1908, the British raided the Gitutu region and confiscated over 8,000 livestock. When Moraa saw Northcate driving away the cattle, she was enraged. Moraa incited the young men saying they were just like women who did not care that their cattle were being taken away. Among the young men who were angered by this admonition by Moraa was her nephew, Otenyo Nyamaterere who conceived a counterattack plan on the British officers as they were marching the livestock out of Bogetutu. Otenyo assembled warriors and with blessings from Moraa, they waylaid the British officers beside the path along which they were riding. Consequently, on 18 January 1908, as Northcote was passing on his horse, behind the police detail accompanying him, Otenyo threw his spear and struck him in the back before he could draw his gun to defend himself. Moraa's incitement to the spearing of Northcote served to ignite armed resistance to British colonial rule in Gusiiland.

This infuriated the British colonialists. In retaliation, they shot and killed a lot of people and also forced, Moraa to use her influence to stop the war and hand over her nephew in exchange for the end of bloodshed. In the end, Moraa chose to save her people. She and the Abagusii elders then gave up Otenyo to the colonial administration. Moraa was also arrested and detained at Kisii police station where she was tortured in an effort to coerce her to submit and cooperate with the colonial administration. She proved recalcitrant and was kept in solidarity confinement. She was later ostracized to Kisimayu. Nevertheless, she never renounced her resolve to say that the white men were strangers on Gusii land and had to leave. Moraa died in 1929 and she is named after many children to this day. Her grave equally deserves to have a monument to show the enormous contribution she made in the struggle for the country's independence.

The Gusii Rain Dance: Ribina

A creative writer once wrote that the sun enables life while the rain grants its safe passage. This artistic expression captures the beauty and abundance of Gusii, a land which experiences relatively sufficient rainfall and sunshine throughout the year. The region boasts of evergreen vegetation, with villages separated from each other with natural landmarks like streams, rivers, valley bottoms and ridges.

It has been noted elsewhere in this book that the volumes of water in rivers and streams within Gusii have reduced drastically over time. Some streams and springs have dried up altogether. Before the 1990s, most springs and rivers in the region used to flood during the peak rainy seasons. This is no longer the case. News of rainwater uprooting vegetation and sweeping animals downstream are not as common as in the past.

We have also stated elsewhere in this book that environmental degradation and climate change are the top culprits as relates to erratic weather patterns as well as the shrinking and diminishing of springs and rivers. This should not imply that our forefathers lived in a land devoid of drought and other natural calamities occasioned by lack of rain or too much of it. The true position is that they too experienced drought, and this led to poor crop yield which eventually led to famine.

It should, however, be noted that the Abagusii people knew that there was a Supreme Being, known as *Engoro*. They knew that *Engoro* had powers over rain, drought, and weather patterns in general. They knew that *Engoro* was the giver, provider, and carer of life. Thus, when the weather turned hostile, they turned to their God in supplication. It thus means that even before the advent of Christianity in the land and the eventual abandonment of traditional religious practices, the Abagusii people believed that they could communicate with their creator, Engoro and he could answer them.

Abagusii may have communicated to *Engoro* on different occasions, but the Ribina dance stood out. *Ribina* was a rain dance that came at the height of a prolonged drought. Led by *abanyibi* (rain makers or "prophets"), *ribina* was meant to ask God to provide rain and rejuvenate the land after a drought. Of all Abanyibi, one Iriasi (Elias) gradually became known across Gusiiland. Iriasi was believed to be an Aphrodite. It is not clear why Iriasi remains the commonest of his class. It could be because he was among the latest before the community got fully immersed in Christianity and other forms of modern ways of worship. Other people argue that Iriasi became famous because he/she was not known to be either male or female.

Lack of rain was regarded as a communal problem. Thus, once it was realized that days were passing without any signs of the return of rain, the community came together in supplication. It should be noted that as much as it was a communal problem, not every member of the community took part in the real performance of the Ribina dance. This was a special task performed by elderly women, at special places set aside for this purpose. The venue of the *ribina* dance was often a raised and flat landscape (*erera*). Such venues included Omobera and Kenyenya in Bomachoge Borabu and Nyagechenche in the South Mugirango Constituency. The dance was also performed at the Manga Hills which lies astride the common border of Nyamira and Kisii counties, and; at Rangenyo and Kiabonyoru in Nyamira County, among other places.

Special arrangements were usually made before the real dance, which mainly happened in the afternoon. The arrangements included communicating with the women who would take part in the dance and young energetic men who would engage in a wrestling match nearby. Although it was considered a spot, wrestling at times ended tragically. One had to be fully prepared to face his opponent. If strength and luck were not on one's side, he could have been killed after a heavy throw or left the scene with critical injuries.

For instance, during our research, we gathered that a wrestling match ended tragically at Nyagechenche when a man from the Abagirango clan fatally threw his challenger from the Abamachoge clan in the air. The man reportedly came down in a thud and died. His clansmen cried homewards carrying the body for burial, while Abagirango had a victory dance back home. Interestingly, the rain fell in torrents that evening and the joy that followed overshadowed the loss of life.

In the past, communication was not as easy as it is today due to technological advancement. Even so, people still communicated amongst themselves and their neighbours using traditional means. For instance, the modes of communication in preparation for the *ribina* dance entailed the blowing of a horn and the hitting of a drum amid verbal declaration of the intended dance and its venue. In response, participants stepped out of their homes with traditional musical instruments (*obokano* and drums) while the women dressed in traditional regalia befitting the occasion went ahead of them. The choreography included wearing special animal skin with sisal ropes that added strong artistic and traditional value to the performance.

Dancers were expected to dance to the same rhythm, but some danced better. As a result, some women who were better dancers became more popular and almost synonymous with the Ribina dance. This was to the extent that they hardly missed the dance whenever and wherever it was held, regardless of the distance from their home. In South Mugirango, it is said that three women (Sabiri, Mogiti and Nyanchama) stood out as the best Ribina dancers. Eventually, a chorus was composed in honour of Sabiri, and it featured during the *ribina* dance across the land. The chorus was sandwiched in the performances and went thus:

> *(Eee Sabiri kumba!) kumbata mogondo are! X2*
>
> *(Eee korwa abakoro!) kumbata mogondo are! X2*

It should be noted that the Abagusii people appreciated the fact that in any competition, there are winners and losers. One such competition was wrestling. This was a masculinity affair and it proved who was more masculine than the other. As a result, when members of Clan A faced Clan B in a wrestling contest, they picked their finest wrestler to face off with the opponent. This was meant to increase the chances of winning the contest and avoid any form of humiliation that followed a loss.

Wrestling had its rules. It was done in an open field devoid of any object that could be converted into a weapon by an overwhelmed participant. The "referee" in this case the rainmaker *Omonyibi* had a special stick *(enungu),* an equivalent of today's trophy. *Omonyibi* was a herbalist of some sort and had to closely guard his herbs and concoctions. The indigenous paraphernalia safeguarded the community from bad omen. The previous winner clan had to surrender the special stick before the contest. It should be appreciated that the wrestlers were not "enemies" in the true sense of the word yet one had to provoke the other for the "fight" to start.

At the initial stages of the face-off, one of the wrestlers was expected to put a stick on the ground and wait for the opponent to touch it. The opponent had to gather sufficient courage to not only touch the stick but remove and throw it away. Just then, a physical confrontation kicked off. One would either be tossed in the air, let to fall, or be tripped. He who fell on his stomach or back was presumed to have lost. The clan whose son won jumped in song and danced homewards with the *enungu*, a justification for their victory. The common win for all of them was the return of rain soon after!

Chapter Seven

Circumcision

This chapter and the next chapter nine on marriage discuss some of the intangible aspects of Abagusii heritage. Intangible heritage is those elements of heritage, which though important, cannot, however, be seen or touched. These include language, songs, myths, stories, dances and other practices that are not physical.

Background

The Abagusii people had and still have four major rites of passage that members undergo in their lives. These are child naming, circumcision, marriage and funeral rites. Whereas some of these rites have declined significantly, circumcision ceremonies have, however, continued to the present day. This may be a result of the role circumcision is seen to play in the socialization and integration of members of the Abagusii community.

There are various theories as to the origins and spread of circumcision. Some anthropologists such as El-Dareer (1978), Giorgis (1981) and Badri and Badri (1990) argue that it is an old practice which dates back to around 500 Before the Common Era (BCE).

In the book of Genesis, chapter 17 verse 2, the Bible records that circumcision, particularly male circumcision was commissioned by God to cement the covenant between God and Abraham. Subsequently, all male descendants of Abraham were supposed to be circumcised when they were eight days old, even though Abraham himself was circumcised when he was very old.

In Africa, the earliest evidence of circumcision has been found on mummies in the Nile Valley. According to Herodotus of Halicarnassus, the Greek researcher and storyteller who wrote in the fifth century BCE and who is said by many to be the world's first historian, Africans whom he broadly classified as Ethiopians and Egyptians, "practice circumcision for the sake of cleanliness, considering it better to be cleanly than comely."

Agatharchides of Cnidus writing in the 2nd century BCE showed that "troglodyte" (cave goers) ethnic groups who may have resided along the African coast of the Red Sea in southern Egypt or near the Gulf of Zula in present-day Eritrea practised circumcision.

In most African communities, initiation was and still is an important integral part of the society. It is a rite of passage since it subjects an individual to a kind of dying, to be re-born under a new personality: a responsible person ready to take up new tasks and responsibilities such as marriage to raise children and defend the community from adversaries, among others. This is what initiation is all about; to introduce an individual into adult life and much more into the world of the Supreme Being (spiritual belonging) and adhering to existing cultural values.

Both Male and female initiation ceremonies were highly valued by the Abagusii people because they were seen as the avenues through which important life lessons such as morality, community values, taboos and customs were imparted to the youth. In other words, it was the time when the youth's identity as Omogusii was created through circumcision; the youth was fully integrated into the life of the family in communion with the ancestors.

Socio-Cultural Reasons

For most anthropologists, initiation ceremonies are multifunctional because on one hand, they can be used to change one's status or they can be used to lessen or eliminate collision in existing social relations (Kenyatta 1978; Van Gennep 1972; Gluckman 1962). Gluckman(1962) further argues that initiation ceremonies can help in differentiating roles in society, especially where people play many roles.

It can be said that, as it has been observed elsewhere, amongst the Abagusii, initiation ceremonies had a communal characteristic and the people developed a sense of identity and belonging within the community. In particular, the ceremonies were seen as a hierarchical structure that led to the social maturity of the members because they signalled a movement of the individual from an old lower status into a new, higher and prestigious social status (Mbithi, 1975).

General Requirements for Circumcision

Before an individual was circumcised, there were various requirements that the initiate must have fulfilled. First for the initiate to qualify he/she, had to attain the pubertal age. Second, the initiate, with the help of their parents, identified a place for seclusion and who their sponsor (*omosegi*) would be. In the case of boys, if they didn't have one, a hut (*esaiga*) had to be put up as the beginning of detachment from their parents.

For the girls, a kitchen house was also constructed for them. It was a custom that circumcised children could not sleep in the same house with their parents; even if the house had many bedrooms. It was still considered taboo for circumcised children to sleep under the same roof as their parents.

Initiation Period

Traditionally, initiation took place between October and December, immediately after the harvest. This period was opportune because food was plenty and therefore the families of the initiates were in the position of holding feasts to celebrate the initiation of their children. However, as a result of school, the initiation time is now mostly in December, though some parents do it in August. Therefore, during the initiation period, a carnival mood swept through Gusiiland.

The circumcision ceremony was an elaborate affair. It started right from the preparation of the initiate and to post-circumcision tutorials that were meant to ground the individuals into youthful and responsible adults who could take their place in society as defenders of self and community.

It is also important to note that circumcisers, *abasari* (for women) and *abakebi* (for men) were a chosen few and they came from specific families. This means that during the sunset days of a circumciser, s/he prepared her/his heir to carry on with it once the old man passed on.

For one to qualify for the rite, the initiate must be a boy or girl of puberty age- about 10 or more years old before he/she could be circumcised. When one came of age, they were guided by young men/women who had already passed the rite on the dos and don'ts in their next phase of life. The guidance provided lessons on how the young man/woman should relate with their parents onwards, members of the opposite sex, the elders, and the larger community in general.

They were told that they were no longer children but young men/women who should walk, talk, and behave like other men/ladies. Young men were also told to be bold and be ready to defend their families and communities against external aggression. Virtues of hard labour and enterprising spirit were also inculcated in them. Girls on the other hand were taught how to prepare meals and generally how to take care of the homes.

It should be noted that this ceremony was communal. Thus, there were mass initiates at any given time. Preparation for initiation included identifying the group of boys/girls who would undergo the cut and those who would be their guides *(abasegi)*. Families also prepared food and local brew that would be consumed during the celebration while the young boys gathered firewood including tree stumps that they would use to light a fire continually during their day in seclusion that lasted a month or so. The families had to agree on who the circumciser would be and where he would be found.

On the eve of the initiation ceremony, young men who had already been circumcised, gathered at the home of the candidate to prepare him. They spoke and grilled him on how he would handle various issues onwards. This session bordered on harassment and ridicule as they humiliated and laughed at the candidate(s) whenever he answered that the older boys did not find appropriate. Further, the initiate was given several tests which included, picking a burning stick from the middle of a burning fire, sitting on stinging needle plants *(rise(amase(pl)/enyanduri)* while naked, as well as standing still for a long time as a sign of discipline.

The candidate was then allowed to sleep, only to be woken up before the roosters crowed. He was then led out of home while naked and led to the river/spring where he was required to dip himself. He was expected to do this each time they came across a river on their way to meet the circumciser. This was a conventional anesthesia so that the boy would not feel pain and bleed much once he got the cut.

The real circumcision was done under a special tree, *omouru/ omosocho*. The circumciser did not have any other surgical equipment, save for a knife that was specially made for this purpose. This was the knife he could use on all the initiates irrespective of their number. Fortunately, at the time, there were no life-threatening diseases like HIV-Aids that were transmitted through contaminated blood.

It should also be noted that as already stated, the candidate did not receive any form of drug to relieve the pain. However, the water immersion worked both as a reliever of pain and an inhibitor of excessive loss of blood. The initiate faced the knife when fully conscious. He was however not allowed to look down but face straight ahead while the circumciser operated on him.

The cut was one-way and happened within seconds. After the cut, the young boy was required to hold his manhood up within two of his fingers until they got home. A scare that manhood would disappear if it was not held made the young men obey this requirement religiously. The holding was meant to prevent excessive bleeding that could occur if the manhood was left to hang.

All the initiates brought before *omokebi* had to patiently wait until he circumcised the last one. He would then lead the delegations in a song dubbed *Esimbore* for a few minutes before he could let them go. The song went as follows:

Oyo-oyo-o-o! X2	Here he is! Here he is!
Omoisia omoke mbororo bwamorire!	The little one is in pain
Omosia omoke ateta, ngina!	The little boy, copulates with his mother
Oyo-oyo-o-o!	He is here! He is here!

For the girls, the women sang different songs but just in the case of boys, though the songs are obscene, they are however educative on acceptable behaviour in society. The socks denigrate untoward behaviour but praise success. The overall emphasis is mostly on moral values such as, without women, there is no life, friends share food and sex relations should be between the circumcised only.

The songs signalled the start of the journey back home. The journey was expected to be slower, dramatic and exciting. There was song and dance with derogatory words being spoken without any fear or shame. The initiates had to be shielded by their seniors in such a way that they could not come into eye contact with curious passers-by and women.

Additionally, it is important to note that the men had to be received along the way by excited and highly charged women including the initiate's mother. The mother usually decorated differently and appeared more excited and energetic than the others. She had to carry a machete or a spear, the two items associated with men and bravely. This meant that she was a proud mother of a boy who had graduated to a man. The men and women were however not allowed to mix but dance and communicate from a distance.

Once at home, the initiates were temporarily taken into a nearby bush where they stayed while merry-making went on in the homestead. The boys were equally served with food in the bush and ate in silence. Towards evening, they were led to the seclusion hut by *Omosegi* who had to enter first and lay a skin on the ground for the initiates to sit on.

Omosegi also lit a traditional ritualistic fire and ensured that he fed it with wood all the time so that it could not go out. The fire was lit using special types of trees like *engoto, omosabakwa, egesiringi and esasi* without using a matchbox. Instead, the fire was lit by rubbing one stick against the other until it sparked and produced fire.

It should be remembered that it was taboo for the fire to go off. It was believed that if it went off, it would spell a bad omen to the young man and the whole family. Importantly, it was believed that this was a sign of a curse including the inability to bear children. Impotence was one of the most dreaded curses as it would halt procreation and extension of a family tree.

On the third day in seclusion, *omosegi* with the help of *omosichi* (an assistant) prepared a bed on which the initiates would sleep onwards. The boys also planted some grass at the entrance of the hut on this day, as a show that it was out of bounds for particular individuals like their mothers. The initiates were also not required to use this door from then on during their stay in seclusion.

During seclusion, the boys were fed well. Even so, they were restricted from going to their parents' hut and having eye contact with them. They were also not required to scream or shout that they were hungry. Instead, they threw sticks and stones on the roof of their parents as a way of passing the message.

During this period of seclusion, only older circumcised boys and girls are allowed to visit the secluded initiates and any other visitor could cause a taboo. It was during this period that initiates were taught their roles as young men in the community and the dos and don'ts of a circumcised man. The initiated boys and girls were also taught the rules of shame *chinsoni*) and respect (*amasikani*). Unlike most communities in Kenya where the circumcised boys and/or girls joined an age set or age group, the circumcised Gusii boys and girls did not join any age set or age group given that the Abagusii lack age sets and age groups.

The seclusion period was meant to enable the wounds to heal. They also got more life skills and advice from Omosegi. However, as they healed, they were free to wander in the bushes where they could kill birds and wild animals such as hares and antelopes. They could also fight with other peers and play, but with a keen eye not to be seen or found by their mothers and aunties.

Near the end of their seclusion, the young boys were subjected to a test that sounded life-threatening but which in reality was not. The ceremony known as *Esubo* entailed the roar of *Enyambumbu/enyabububu* (this was a pot full of water buried under the ground, filled and tied with an animal hide at the top). This object was skillfully twisted to make a scaring roar like a lion in darkness. The sound emanating from it was so scary that some attendees were scared to the bones. Remaining calm at this hour was considered to be the hallmark of courage. This matriculation ritual was the climax of the boys' stay in seclusion.

Further, the boys were made to take an oath never to divulge secrets of this unique ceremony. They were to vow that they would not disclose any information to uncircumcised boys, girls, and mothers about what they went through to become men. This "oathing" was also meant to prepare them for the fact that not every piece of information was meant for consumption by everybody (some of the information was supposed to be classified). Indeed, even to this day, although many underwent the ceremony, they can hardly tell the journey in detail. The oath still stands, so to say.

To recap it all, it can be said that seclusion was an important part of initiation; it actualized the meaning of initiation. It was during seclusion that the initiates were schooled in the critical cultural aspects of the community and told the pertinent secrets of life. As already stated, for instance, there was the *esuguta* grass (*imperata cyclindrica*) planting ceremony that symbolized the health of the initiates. The planting of the grass near the door of the initiate's hut was done on the third day after the operation by the circumcisor. The grass was collected from the bush by those already initiated and brought to the seclusion hut and planted indoors and watered by the initiates; if it dried up, that was interpreted to mean a bad omen. As the grass grew and remained healthy, it was believed that the initiate would also in the future be healthy and bring forth healthy children.

Therefore, while the *esuguta ceremony* was meant to symbolize the continuity of life and to have the initiates exercise a sense of responsibility; the *esubo* ceremony i.e., the supposed roaring of a lion was on the other hand, used to test the courage of the initiates.

By the time the initiates came out of seclusion, they had left fear and cowardice behind. They were expected to confront life challenges without fear and with dedicated focus. They were no longer children but adults who should take bold steps and make wise decisions for the good of their families, the community, and themselves.

As already presented, circumcision is one of the ceremonies that have withstood the test of time, albeit with tremendous adulterations. It has gradually metamorphosed into a surgical procedure for health reasons. The cultural aspect has been delinked from circumcision. Presently, most workers in the medical field can conduct the cut, successfully, because it has been medicalized. This is to the extent that once cut, the boy can stay at the hospital until he heals or go and stay under the same roof with his parents for the healing to take place.

Secondly, it is now clear that there is not much cultural and ritualistic attachment to circumcision. Thus, there is no elaborate preparation of the boys for this phase of life. There is also little focus on a boy's age since some get circumcised when they are barely five years old. These are still children in the real meaning of the word and have not matured in their minds and character to differentiate and/or identify themselves with other men.

For the girls, as a result of the campaigns by many women activists, this rite of passage is now being called Female Genital Mutilation (FGM) and has been said to be associated with many health challenges that women face especially when giving birth. Consequently, the Kenya government has banned the practice. That notwithstanding, there are some families, both educated and uneducated who are secretly, with surprisingly with the assistance of some medical professionals, still carrying out the practice.

We also noted that the ceremony happened in August. Abagusii people were particular about this because this was a month of plenty. This was the time they had a bumper harvest and food was not a problem. Following the introduction and uptake of formal education and emphasis on the education calendar, the ceremony was for some time shifted to December. This was to allow would-be initiates to finish their year of study before they could return home to undergo the cut. It should also be noted that in the past, boys were cut under a special tree *(omwobo/omosocho)* which was considered to be sacred amongst Abagusii. Presently, circumcision is done at the hospital and in any month of the year.

The element of the usage of natural anesthesia, harassment and grilling of the initiates has also fizzled out over time. Presently, the procedure is done using surgical knives scissors and pain relievers. The wound is also stitched or sprinkled with disinfectants to heal quickly. This was unheard of in the past. Importantly, these sets of surgical items are used for one client and disposed of. This is critical news, particularly in the interest of taming the spread of diseases like HIV-Aids.

Omosari (Circumciser)

The *omosari/omokebi* was a qualified operator and had to be an elderly man, a father of children who had also been initiated. The *omosari/omokebi* was, however, an ordinary person, who rose from the lineage of *abasari/abakebi* (circumcisers) or anyone who felt that he had a calling to this cultural duty and made it known to the community, who in turn anointed him to do so. Currently many qualify as circumcisers, especially those in the medical field because circumcision has been secularized and commercialized.

The main traditional circumcision tool was a homemade knife but presently this has been replaced with a pair of scissors and other accessories that are preferred by the medical practitioners who have now taken over the role of traditional circumcisers.

At the end of the exercise, the circumciser was paid his dues after which he pitched the celebration song *"esimbore"* (sacred song), to release the initiates to go back to their homes. Orphaned children, as well as those initiates who were born after a number of their brothers and sisters had died *"abatakerwa"* (ones dedicated to the ancestral spirits), were circumcised free of charge. This was because they were considered an unfortunate group who required free services.

The Ritualistic Fire

After arriving home and being taken to the seclusion hut, the first act to be performed was the lighting of the ritualistic fire. The fire was to be kept burning throughout the entire seclusion period. This fire was lit through drilling using a dry hard stick against the dry wood of *engoto* tree. To facilitate the lighting of the fire, dry cow-dung *(orosiriri)* was applied to the hole made by the stick over the *engoto*. The ritualistic fire was kept burning day and night because if it went off, it was believed that later in life the initiate would face calamities. For instance, one may not be able to bear children unless a sacrifice is offered (a goat was slaughtered; this sacrifice was called *ogosegwa kwomorero*- appeasing the fire) to appease the ancestral spirits. It was strongly held among the Gusii people that fire is a symbol of fertility.

As a result of the sensitivity of the ritualistic fire, both the sponsors and the initiates were entreated to ensure that the fire never went off during the period of seclusion. Further, before the initiation ceremony, the initiates were supposed to gather enough firewood (*ebitugi*) that they would use to keep the fire burning. However, the families of the initiates also ensured that they provided enough firewood during seclusion to ensure that the initiates never ran out of it.

The normal practice was that initiates from the same extended family used to share the same seclusion hut. This was mainly done for practical reasons such as ensuring that the initiates were fed properly since it was an expensive undertaking to feed the initiates, but when two or three families came together, it became cheaper. Further, the sharing of the same hut was meant to instill communal ideals and discourage individualistic tendencies.

End of Seclusion (Ekiarokio or Korua Nyomba)

After healing, and therefore end of seclusion, several things were carried out to prepare the initiates for the next phase of their life. First, on the eve of the graduation, the initiates were taught about the use of various medicinal herbs and how to behave as adult males or females in the community. It should be noted that this was the only period since the initiation process began, that the initiate was treated in a friendly manner, a gesture that meant that the initiate was now crossing over to adulthood.

On the actual graduation day, very early in the morning, the initiates were taken by their sponsors to the river for a bath after which they could dress in new clothes. As the initiates were busy preparing themselves for their graduation (*korua nyomba*), the rest of the family members were also busy preparing a feast for community members to welcome the initiates into the community.

After officially coming out of seclusion, each initiate had to be blessed by his/her father using milk and beer. Each father of the initiate was offered milk and beer by the respective sponsor; the father sipped a little milk and beer in turns and spat on the initiate as he uttered words of blessings and prosperity. This blessing practically marked the end of seclusion and years of childhood. At this juncture, the *esuguta* grass was uprooted from indoors and planted outside. This now marked the transition of the initiate from childhood to adulthood.

Respect

After initiation, both boys and girls were now taken to be adults and they were therefore taught and expected to exhibit respect (*chinsoni*) to their parents and all other people in the community. For instance, boys were expected to exhibit *chinsoni* values to their mothers by refraining from entering their mother's bedrooms and avoiding shaking hands with them. They were also required not to sit near the fireplace when the mother was cooking, lest the mother's skirt could pull up and the boy could see her thighs. Girls were also expected to show *nsoni,* particularly to their fathers. Girls were, however, allowed to enter their parents' bedrooms but only during the absence of their fathers.

Parents were also required to reciprocate this respect. For fathers, there were various ways to show *chinsoni* to their children. For instance, a father could not enter his married son's house nor was he allowed to be present at the place where his son's wife was giving birth. Although the mother was allowed to enter her married son's house, she, however, could not go beyond the sitting room.

Chapter Eight

Marriage and its Sanctity in Gusii

Society in general abhors and condemns infidelity in marriage. As a result, many communities have put in place mechanisms for dealing with infidelity when it occurs. For instance, in the Republic of Guinea, a husband was allowed to kill or abuse a wife for real or imagined infidelity (Anoko, 2008). According to the Bible, the penalty for an adulterous Jewish person was stoning to death (New International Version, Leviticus, 20:10). Equally in Islam stoning to death has been and still is a punishment for those involved in infidelity (Islamic Sharia Law, 2015).

Among the Abagusii, sex outside marriage could only be permitted because of the death of one's spouse and the approval by the community for the widow to be inherited. The community had to approve that a particular man inherits a widow after meeting a clear criterion that locked out other potential inheritors. Wife inheritance was particularly for childbearing purposes and perpetuation of the departed man's family line. The man who inherited another man's wife did not count the offspring from the relationship as his but the dead man's.

There were also rare incidences where the community learnt that although married, one was impotent. Impotence was considered a curse and the elders could come together to meditate and offer sacrifices in a bid to reverse the curse. It was believed that indeed, offering sacrifices would reverse one's impotence so that he bears children. But there were incidences where one could not impregnate his wife even after the sacrifices. To save face, elders could organize behind his back and entice one's wife to deliberately wander in the bush where they would have set a selected young man to waylay her. The two could then "forcibly" have a sexual encounter that would culminate into pregnancy and eventual delivery of a baby. The wife was not expected to tell anybody of that encounter, not even her husband, only to save the marriage. This was rather awkward but was justifiably so that the real husband counted the children born out of such arrangement as biologically his.

Away from these extreme cases, marriage was considered a sacred relationship and sex before marriage was unheard of; infidelity in marriage was a great abomination. There were safeguards to ensure marriages remained sacred. These included if it was a woman involved, sending her away to her home to bring a goat as a fine.

Another form of punishment which was not administered by any human being but by the ancestral spirits was known as *amasangia* (Ayako, 2020). *Amasangia* were effective only when blood or sickness was involved and occurred under certain situations.

One of these circumstances was if an adulterous spouse fell ill and the other spouse fed or served her/him with meat, the sick spouse would die. Further, if the person committing adultery with the spouse came to see the sick spouse, this could also lead to the death of the sick person or if a woman was unfaithful and the husband crossed over her blood while giving birth, the unfaithful wife got an attack and passed on.

Immediately the husband crossed the blood a chain of events occurred. One, the woman started to sweat, she stretched herself slowly, became elastic, and eventually passed on. If, however, quick action was taken and a traditional remedy known as *rirongo* was administered, she could not die. Secondly, if a wife was unwell and an adulterous husband decided to slaughter a goat for her, to quicken her recovery, she could pass on mysteriously because of sharing blood from the goat.

Amasangia was no respecter of amorous husbands. Such a man stood the risk of getting exposed if he was fed by his wife during the time of sickness. It was said that the act of being fed by his wife would trigger unusual and abnormal swelling of his manhood. This would compel him to testify that he had cheated on someone's wife. The affected couples would then come together to be cleansed.

Safeguards Against *Amasangia*

To avoid being attacked by *amasangia* some precautionary measures were carried out by the adulterous individual early before the illicit relationship was known or before any event that could cause an attack could occur. The precaution involved the cheating partner making sure that his or her spouse had common food with the one he or she was having an affair with. They ate from the same container. To quote Mokua et al (2022:47):

> *"If* a woman was unfaithful, she could invite the man they had an affair with to her home. This was after making sure that she had made this man a friend to the husband or created a situation which could make them meet at mealtime. She could cook a meal or drink, then put some concoction which was called *rirongo* in it. Once they shared this food which contained this concoction, *amasangia* could not kill them in future even if they set eyes on each other in the event one was sick or giving birth."

What about polygamous marriage?

Our informants told us that *amasangia* did not affect spouses in a polygamous marriage because in such a situation the marriage process had been followed. However, if a polygamous man had sexual affairs outside his legally married wife, *amasangia* could still lead to death. The man was therefore required to strictly remain faithful to his wives.

Remedy for *amasangia*

Amasangia could kill very quickly. However, if it was realized fast enough that *amasangia* may be the cause of a sudden change in the health condition of the victim and necessary interventions undertaken, death could be averted. The earliest first aid measure to be undertaken before death occurred was to make the victim (man or woman who was likely to die) cross over a dog. Abagusii took a dog as an animal with no morals and therefore an amorous individual was equated to having dog-like characters. After this first aid, the process of treatment commenced which involved the victim or one whose life was in danger being given a special concoction that was known *as rirongo.*

Not everybody could prepare this concoction but a woman who had reached menopause (*omokungu obutire korwa konyora abana*). She made this concoction from a combination of varied soils gotten from numerous areas that included: a heap of soil made by a mole (*ribusio rieng'uko*), ant hill soil (*ribusio riechimonyo*), soil taken from a junction where two roads/paths cross each other (*amaroba korwa amatabekania*), termite hill soil (*ekegege*), cray from a swamp (*esike ye tente*), faeces of an antbear (*amabi ye eguto*), silt heaped due to erosion caused by rain (*amaroba yo omogoko*) and intestine waste of a sheep (*euura ye eng'ondi*). The components were mixed and then they were dried on a hide (*egesero*). When an attack occurred, the victim was given the concoction to sip after which he/she recovered from the attack.

Apart from human beings, the concoction was given to animals like cows to protect them from an evil eye. According to Moronya (2013), however, *rirongo* was always made ready and kept for any eventuality that *amasangia* attack, may take place. This may indicate that the community was cognizant of the fact that human beings are prone to amorous behaviour.

However, there were situations where a woman cheated and got scot-free. In other words, there were times when one could cheat behind her partner without being caught; this happened especially if none of the spouses got sick and therefore there was no opportunity for the *amasingia* to happen. Unfortunately, however, a time of reckoning had to come in the fullness of time. This happened when the husband died. If such a woman wanted to live long alongside her children without being haunted by the spirits of the departed husband, she did not have an option apart from testifying to the elders that she had been cheating in her marriage. This confession, however, had to be made before the burial of the husband. After the testimony, the elders prepared the *rirongo* and placed it on the corpse's cold hand and ordered the adulterous wife to consume it. It was a rather painful and shameful experience but she had to do it for the sake of peace with the departed husband otherwise she would follow him to the grave.

Adultery and Truth: *Ogosangia Abatomani*

Sometimes, it could be that an adulterous person shows signs of *amasangia* attack, especially if they are sharing a meal with the person whose spouse they have been cheating with. In that case, it was essential for the adulterous person to come out and say the truth. Consequent to the admission, the process of treating the *amasangia* began.

The adulterer was required to provide a goat which was slaughtered; the bowels were removed and mixed with honey and then the adulterer and the spouse of the other adulterous person were given the mixture to eat. Then the adulterous couple were brought together and made to kneel with stretched-open palms.

Pieces of bowels mixed with *rirongo* were placed on their palms. They seeped the mixture like dogs using their tongues. Then, they were given the thigh bone from the slain goat which the adulterous couple held, each from one side. They cut it into two pieces with each of them taking one part. They also chewed the muscles (*emenyika*).

By strictly adhering to the rules *amasangia* could be averted. Hence, it was assumed that reconciliation had been realized. The entire procedure was so demanding and tedious that individuals favoured maintaining faithfulness. In essence, therefore, it should be noted that *Amasangia* was meant to safeguard marriages and ensure they stayed sacrosanct.

Chapter Nine

Gusii Homestead

Background

After initiation into adulthood, the next step for young adults was marriage. When one got married, a man was supposed to move away from his parents' homestead and set up his homestead (*omochie oye*) which could either be near or further away from his parent's homestead, depending on the size of the land of his father as well as the size of land that his father has bequeathed him.

Among the Gusii people, the homestead was experienced by its inhabitants as a unit of economic expansion and social control. The behaviour of the individual vis-a-vis other members of society was expressed starting from the homestead onwards to the broader community. Thus for instance, the senior wife (first wife) of a man had always her house built at the centre of the homestead, while those of her co-wives were built to the right and left of her hut respectively. Even when the houses are not in the same compound, always the house of the first wife would be constructed on the right side of the man's farm. Whenever a visitor came to the homestead he knew how to behave towards the women he found at those houses by just observing their pattern. This same kind of structuring of huts was extended into the inside of the individual houses where the ordering of space within the house also reflected the relationship between the various members of that house. For example, the location of the hearth stones was in such a way that a man knew where to sit vis-a-vis the women in the house.

In this regard, the Abagusii house was divided into two rooms. A woman's room (*nyomba ime*) in which cooking and sleeping took place and, a man's room (*eero*) in which male entertainment such as beer drinking and most other domestic rituals took place.

A man's room was always on the right-hand side and the woman's room on the left. This was depicted from the placement of the doors. The house had two doors, the first one faced the cattle kraal and entered directly into the man's room and this was usually used by the man and his relatives. This door was called the door of the cattle kraal (*egesieri kia bweri*). It signified the fact that it was the role of the man to look after and protect the family's livestock.

The second door entered directly into the woman's room and was used by the wife and her friends. It was called *egesieri kia gesaku*. It signified that the women were the ones who gave birth to the family children. But if he wished, the husband could use this door as well; and indeed in most cases, this is the door that was used frequently. What the arrangement of the doors shows is the strong attachment that the Abagusii had to the patrilineal lineage and the role that cattle played in the enhancement of the lineage.

The cattle were used to pay bride price to bring more women into the village and thus get more children, therefore ensuring the survival of the lineage. It was thus important that the cattle be closely guarded by members of the lineage, especially the men.

The patterning of the house also shows Abagusii's attitude towards women. They were seen not only as outsiders- who should not use the lineage's door and thus come directly into contact with the cattle which were important in the continuity of the lineage, but also that they were inferior to the men and should always be in the shadow or background of men. This inferiority of women is nowhere depicted well than in the way things were spatially ordered within the house and the whole homestead in general.

All items that were made by women such as pots and baskets were usually stored in the woman's room or in the ceiling *(irongo)* which was supposed to be used exclusively by the woman. On the other hand, all male-made items such as hoes, machetes and baskets, were stored in the men's room. This is even though in their daily life, these tools were either used mostly by women, for instance, the hoes and baskets, or by men who used the pots for beer drinking.

Gusii Homestead

Military Strategy

a. Fortifications *(Chindwaki and Chiburi)*

The history of the Abagusii community may not be fully understood without appreciating the fact that its greatest threat to their survival was repeated and bloody attacks by their neighbours. After they migrated from their supposed homeland, the first settlement for the Abagusii in Nyanza was at Yimbo where they may have stayed for two generations (Ndeda 2019).

The Gusii people were initially a cattle-keeping community but between 1520 and 1755, as they were setting down to settle in the Lake Victoria basin area, their institutions underwent a dramatic transformation. First, they came into contact with the initial wave of cattle-keeping Luo migrants and this made the Abagusii move away from Yimbo and eventually settle in the Kano Plains (Ochieng' 1974b: 13, Aberi 2009).

According to Ng`ang`a (2006), the movement of Abagusii out of the Kano plains happened sometime in 1755 when the incoming Luo migrants forced the Abagusii to move to Kabianga in the present Kericho County, where they did not stay for long because the place was wet and cold most of the time, but more importantly, their staple food crops such as millet and pumpkins as well as livestock could not do well which led to an outbreak of famine that killed many people (Ndeda 2019, Ochieng' & Maxon 1992). The Gusii had to make a strategic pronouncement that *"kabianga togende"* meaning "since things have refused, let us go". Kabianga thus became the name of the place to this day. In addition, the Kipsigis and Maasai constantly attacked them. This was the period between 1789 and 1809.

Even after moving away and settling in their present homeland, the Abagusii found themselves surrounded by three Nilotic-speaking communities, the Maasai, the Kipsigis and the Luo. These communities were a major threat to Abagusii, due to their regular attacks to raid for cattle. For instance, in 1892, there was a fierce battle between the Kipsigis and most of the Abagusii clans (Silberschmidt 1999).

According to Orchardson (1971) among the Kipsigis, raiding of cattle was a time sports event and was institutionalized. Cattle theft from outside the community was the objective of their active lives and a test of their military prowess.

The Gusii community was to a large extent on the receiving end because of its small population. Their weaponry included spears, slings, poisoned arrows and shields which they used for self-defence. Their neighbours had the same weapons but were more skilled at the battlefront and were bigger in number. The Gusii community also relied on curses *(ebiranya)* where their prophets and seers cursed that their enemy be subdued. Such prophets included Sakagwa whose prophecies particularly as relating to triumph against the enemy were taken with seriousness by members of the community.

As a result of these frequent raids, the Abagusii community had to find a way to survive and overcome the enemy who was determined not only to reduce their livestock but equally take over their land. It was for this reason that young men were always positioned at strategic hilltops to blow an alarm (horn - *egetureria*) and alert people in the adjacent villages in case there was an approaching enemy. The community warriors could then take strategic positions and confront the enemy.

Further, to escape from consistent raids from the Kipsigis and Maasai, the members of the Abagusii community identified caves, low-lying valleys and escarpments surrounded by slopes where they could hide with their livestock. The community also devised other methods that would make it more cumbersome and riskier for their enemies to succeed in their ill missions. This is how the Abagusii eventually decided to build heavy stone fortifications called *chindwaki* (plural) or (*orwaki*, singular) around their villages that were boosted on the outside by deep trenches (*chiburi*) (Achoki 2020).

According to Gusii elders, at night all cattle were brought into the fortifications while men and warriors slept outside to keep an eye over the animals. *Orwaki* was a long stone wall that "ring-fenced" the homesteads and ensured that the homestead could only be accessed through one entrance. These two defensive strategies worked very well in keeping the enemy away, particularly when they got combined.

Clans that formed the Gusii community also appreciated the fact that they were small in number and were likely to be exterminated from the face of the earth if they clang to their clans. They realized that the only solution to their survival was unity of purpose and the adoption of military strategies that could work in their favour.

Whenever the enemies struck, they had to confront them as a singular community. Over time, it emerged that Gusii warriors got smarter at the war front. The Osaosao battle in which Kipsigis raiders were killed to a man stands out to be one of the greatest battles ever won by Gusii warriors against their neighbours. At present, one cannot find a trace of Chindwaki and Chiburi anywhere in Gusiiland.

Though their traces have been obliterated by farming and other construction works, Chindwaki and Chiburi were found in places like Nyansara, Misesi and Kineni (Gekomoni) among other areas. Other places where there are claims of *chindwaki* include Bonyaiguba near Miruka market not far from Gekomoni, Matongo area which is supposed to be the first orwaki to be built and Ekerenyo, near the present chief's camp. There is, however, no evidence of these fortifications. However, where some places bear the name "Orwaki" which is the singular form of Chindwaki.

Description of Orwaki at Gekomoni in Nyamira County

Though now destroyed by farming activities, this *orwaki* was located at Gekomoni (Kineni) which is located on the east of Rangenyo Mission of West Mugirango constituency in Nyamira County.

Originally *orwaki* was a stockade of stones cemented together with mud. It seems that the stockade was subjected to fire after the completion of the structure to harden the stones. The whole structure was about eight to ten feet high. The outside of the stockade had a deep trench (eburi) that was seven to nine feet deep. Oral traditions indicate that a tree was used as a watchtower and at night it was occupied by a sentry who blew a horn whenever he saw anything suspicious. The wall was built on the side of a hill which made it extremely difficult for any attacker to settle.

Some people claim that this wall may have been built after the battle of Mogori (Osaosao); suppose this is the case, then this fortification may have been built in the 1890s. This wall was used continually until the coming of the Europeans to the area in the 1900s.

b. The Osaosao/Mogori Battle

The epic Osaosao/Mogori battle pitying Gusii warriors against their adversaries from the Kipsigis side in 1896 was the bloodiest of all. It was the turning point of the Gusii people as a distinct ethnic community, having triumphed against their troublesome and merciless neighbours.

The genesis of the Osaosao war can be traced as said above, to around the 1750s when the Abagusii were living in the Belgut area of today's Kericho County. While there, the Abagusii were under constant attacks from the Kipsigis and this greatly affected their socio-economic and political life. These attacks, for instance, couldn't allow the Abagusii to till and sow crops the right season thus leading to poor harvests and famines which were followed by diseases.

Some of the diseases that they and their livestock suffered at Kabianga included *enyamoko* (smallpox) and *entira* (anthrax) whose causes they blamed on Kalenjin invaders. When later, the *abamanyi* (the Isiria Maasai) joined the raids, the Abagusii were forced to move out of Kabianga and attempted to settle between Litein and Sotik.

Towards the end of the 18th Century, the Gusii and the Lumbwa (a section of the Kipsigis) clashed at the battle of Chemoiben near Litein in which the Abagusii were badly defeated. The Abagusii fled in different directions, some to present-day Manga, while the majority fled towards Sotik where some Abagusii clans were assimilated by the Kipsigis.

Despite fleeing, the Kipsigis continued pursuing the Abagusii. Consequently, in around 1780 another battle, now known as the battle of Ng'oina between the two communities took place at Ngoina. The Abagusii who, however, had been forewarned of an impending attack were not caught by surprise when the attack occurred. They had prepared well and thus they were ready to confront the Kipsigis (Langat 1969). In spite of the loss, the Kipsigis continued to raid Abagusii forcing them to move further south to Gelegele, Ikorongo, and into Riokebirio and Ngararo in present-day Maasailand where the Abagusii encountered the Isiria Maasai.

In 1840, the two communities fought the battle of Migori (not to be confused with the battle of Mogori) in which the Abagusii were badly defeated and fled in different directions. Some Abagusii groups fled to Getembe and Manga escarpment where they rejoined the other Abagusii groups who had settled there earlier after moving from Kabianga. Other Abagusii groups fled to Kurialand and Luoland where they were absorbed by the existing people, mainly the Luo.

The Maasai followed their victory by annexing huge chunks of Gusii land. Meanwhile, on the eastern section of the Gusii, the Kipsigis took advantage of Gusii's military weakness to expand as far as Keroka and Kegati. According to Akama (2006:36), "the Kipsigis started to make incursions into the Gusii villages that were situated at the frontier areas of Isecha to the North of the Manga hills, while the Maasai cattle raiders started attacking outlying Gusii villages in Nyagoe forest." The Gusii were therefore threatened by the Maasai from the South, the Luo in the North, and the Kipsigis in the East.

As a result of their small numbers, and the constant raids from their neighbours, the Abagusii, after moving from Kabianga, confined themselves to a small section of today's Gusiiland. They avoided the upper side of Gusii which forms Nyamira County. Their fears were based on the fact that the menacing and daring

Kipsigis raiders were determined to wipe them from the face of the earth.

According to local narratives, in 1895 a severe disease, now known to have been rinderpest, had attacked and killed thousands of cattle of the Kipsigis. The rinderpest pandemic made many Kipsigis whose source of livelihood was cattle destitute.

Further, according to Gusii oral traditions, 1889 was their year of abundance; apart from a bumper harvest of Millet, sorghum, pumpkins, and bananas in Gusiiland, wild fruits, mushrooms and wild game were seen everywhere in Gusii. Unfortunately, the information about the availability of abundant food in Gusiiland reached the enemy – the Kipsigis, who intensified their cattle raids on the Gusii.

The Gusii elders aware that the Kipsigis may attack them again, approached their seers (*abakumi- omokumi-singular)* (men who had powers to spell a curse) and *ababani* (prophets). At this time, Nyakundi, then leader of the Abagetutu clan, was the senior most *omokumi* while Sakagwa was the seer. Irked with the worsening situation, Nyakundi summoned his peers from all clans of Gusii for a meeting. He also looped in the community's prophetic leader, Sakagwa Ng'iti.

After quickly analyzing the situation, Sakagwa summed the cause of Gusii's failures in war as a lack of unity among Abagusii clans. Sakawa then led the elders to "Ngoro ya Mwaga" and had them solemnly swear to go to war once and for all against the Kipsigis. After offering sacrifices, Sakagwa "planted" strong charms called *"ebiranya"* at Mote Momwamu to enable the Gusii to win the war decisively.

The gospel of Gusii unity was taken by the elders throughout Gusiiland. Patriotic songs were composed to motivate the people. One such song went as follows:

Maera ominto, Maera	Maera my sibling, Maera
Bitunwa Biria, Maera	those nice hills, Maera
Bikorekaine, Maera	intertwined hills, Maera
Maemba Nkongo, Maera	Plentiful millet, Maera

Meanwhile, word had reached the Kipsigis of plenty of agricultural resources that abounded in Gusiiland (Rutto, 2016). Notwithstanding information reaching the Kipsigis about Gusii's war preparedness, the Kipsigis went ahead with their invasion preparations. Langat (1969) observes that because of their past victorious against the Gusii, the Kipsigis developed a false sense of invincibility against the Gusii. Being sure of victory, the Kipsigis prepared for a great raid on the Gusii, young boys were enlisted to drive the livestock home while the women were given the task of carrying home the captured stores of food.

The raiding party under the leadership of Malabun arap Makiche started their onslaught from Sotik. This team was joined at Buret by the team led by Chesengeny arap Koborok. While the warriors were from the Kipkoimet and Sawe generation age-sets, the boys on the other hand were of the Tobari subset.

Other subsets that participated in the war included the Kipsilchoget, and Kebebucha. Kimasiba, Kiboloeng and Kiptermesendet (Komma, 1992). It has been said that Kalenjin elders, medicine men and diviners strongly warned against the raid but the young men could not listen. Further, according to Komma (1992), no sacrifices to the gods nor divinations were carried out as usually was the custom before launching a major cattle raid. It has also been said that during their march to Gusiiland, the vultures kept cycling the raiders overhead.

In African cultures, vultures are regarded as harbingers of death. This caused the two commanders, Malabun and Chesengeny to differ over whether they should postpone the raid. Malabun however, would not listen to any advice and the raiding march to Gusiiland continued.

Amongst the Gusii meanwhile, Sakagwa knew of the impending raid quickly assembled warriors and put in place a new military strategy which the Kalenjin warriors had never encountered before. One of the methods he employed was making the Gusii warriors retreat and organize a muted defence strategy.

Consequently, when the raiders first attacked in North Mugirango, the Gusii put up a muted resistance while retreating towards the strategic Manga Escarpment. The Kalenjin raiders burnt houses and captured old and sickly cows. It is at Manga Escarpment that the Kalenjin warriors killed their first war victims – Omariba and Omabeche – and still, there was no resistance. It is against this situation of Gusii restraint that the Kalenjin warriors got a false sense of winning the war against the

Gusii Komma (1992:7) argues that "in Mogori war (OsaoSao war), the Kipsigis won small battles successfully in the beginning and plundered as they wished to make major advances.

The Kipsigis continued on the offensive and invaded too deeply into Gusiiland." The muted Abagusii resistance aroused the suspicion of one of the Kalenjin commanders, Chesengeny arap Kaborok who suggested to the other commanders that they should withdraw and call off the raid. Malabum arap Makiche refused and in fact, most of Chesengeny's warriors deserted and joined Malabun. Chesengeny managed to escape back to Kalenjinland with a few warriors through Maasai territory. Meanwhile, Malabun now the undisputed leader continued with his warriors to invade the Luo without realizing that prophet Sakagwa of the Gusii had created a "safe passage" for them.

In Luoland however, things did not go according to plan. The Luo, who were not known to fight at night, this time gallantly fought the whole night. In the morning the huge Kalenjin force counted their losses and fled to the Mogori area; their large numbers spreading as far as the Manga Escarpment. According to Gusii's oral tradition, Gusii warriors were under strict instructions from Sakagwa not to attack until he gave his orders. At nine o'clock in the morning, when the tired and hungry Kalenjin warriors started searching for wild berries (*chinkomoni* and *chinkenene*), others were trying to catch precious little sleep, and Sakagwa gave the order for the attack.

What happened next was a human slaughter of tens of thousands of Kalenjin warriors whose whole story has never come to light, intentionally or otherwise. The entire invading force, together with Malabun the supreme commander, was annihilated.

According to Gusii's oral tradition, by the time the war was over in the late afternoon, the water of the two rivers, River OsaoSao and River Echarachani (Mogori) – had turned red overflowing with Kalenjin blood. Piles and piles of human remains were lying on the river banks. According to the residents of the area, heaps of human skeletons were visible, as recently as the late 1990s.

It is believed that *ebiranya* (curses) played a critical role in the success of the Osaosao battle. Kipsigis warriors were subdued to surrender but this did not stop Gusii warriors from ensuring that they did not return to their home with their lives. Those who lay down and pretended that they were already dead were beheaded.

The Osaosao battle was a major drawback to the Kipsigis community. The number of their young people was reduced to almost zero. The battle left behind several young widows in Kipsigis land. To rescue the situation, elders decided that young boys in their community be circumcised to inherit the widows and help replenish the community's numbers. According to several Gusii elders, some young Gusii men also crossed over to Kipsigis land, inherited the widowed wives and fathered several children. For this reason, members of the Kipsigis community residing in the lower parts of Kericho County, for instance, Litein trace their roots to some lineages in Kisii. they also refer to the Gusii as *Gamama* (uncles).

For the Gusii community, Osaosao was a major win. They were now sure that there was no formidable force from the Kipsigis side to fear. They now moved to occupy the part of their land that had been deserted. Many took up land in the present day North Mugirango, West Mugirango and the upper part of Kitutu. This battle is ingrained in the memories of both communities. However, while it evokes sad memories for the Kipsigis, some members of the Gusii community think that due to outright provocation, the battle was inevitable as much as it led to the loss of lives whose number is still unknown.

The scene of this battle is a stone-throw away from the Kisii-Homa-Bay common border. However, there is nothing that one can attach to the battle. The stones in River Osaosao upon which water loudly flows downstream, the sounds of birds that sing from the trees and the Nyakeyo-Nyamokenye murram road that was a mere path intertwined in bushes over a century ago cannot give one an inkling of the epic battle.

Chapter Ten

Summary and Future Works

This book has briefly identified some of the most important Gusii heritage places in both Kisii and Nyamira Counties and their associated intangible elements. This is in addition to some cultural practices that buttressed the lives of Abagusii. It has shown that Abagusii people had an intertwining relationship with their heritage places as these places played an important role in the health of the community. The study has shown that these heritage places enabled the community to establish an equilibrium between people and nature. This enabled the community to build a knowledge system that intertwines nature and culture and made the community build capacities in all spheres of life- economic, social and religious that enabled the sustenance of the community.

It is also worth noting that the Abagusii people considered heritage places in the totality of the landscape I which they were situated. That the areas within which these heritage places are situated were valued in their totality and not that particular place where the heritage place is situated. Therefore, if it is *Ngoro a Mwaga* in Manga escarpment for instance, all the adjoining landscape was protected from destruction as it was believed to be the homestead of the spirits that protected the sacred place.

Heritage is a devolved function. It is therefore important that the county governments of Kisii and Nyamira, come up with a heritage policy that will enable the protection, conservation and preservation of all heritage places in their jurisdiction. The policy should give guidelines on how places can be graded into various levels of value; those local (village), ward and county values and levels of their protection. The policy will also set out the level of involvement of the community in the management of these places and if, the places are earning income, how this income can be shared with the community.

Within the community, some people have movable objects that are important cultural objects. In most cases, however, these objects are not well kept and some of them have or are deteriorating and their information- both in the material used to make them and how they were used, will disappear. There is a need therefore for the two county governments to come together and establish a county museum that will conserve, preserve and exhibit these objects to the public. The museum can also collaborate with institutions like Kisii University to carry out further research on the various aspects of Abagusii culture that have not been covered in this book.

Development of these sites stands to benefit not just the community of Abagusii but will contribute to the country's national and world heritage. And therein lies some of its potential: connecting people across the world through the sharing of experiences especially with the use of technology or via heritage tourism programmes and exchanges.

References

Aberi George E. 2009. *Influence of Gendered Linguistic Images on Girl Education: A Case Study of Southern Kisii District, Kenya.* Master of Arts in English Language and Linguistics, Njoro: Egerton University, October 2009.

Achoki G. N. 2020. The emergence of Abagusii diaspora in Kenya's south rift, 1895-2007: Opportunities and challenges.MA thesis Masinde Muliro University of Science and Technology.

Akama S. and Maxon (eds). 2006. *Ethnography of the Gusii of Western Kenya:* A Vanishing Cultural Heritage, Edwin Mellen Press, Queenston Canada.

Ambler, Charles H. 1989. The Renovation of Custom in Colonial Kenya: the 1932 Generation Succession Ceremonies in Embu. *The Journal of African History.* **30** (1): 139 156. doi:10.1017/s0021853700030929.

Anoko, Juliene N. 2008. *Gender Inequality in the Protected France Areas of West Africa.* France: UCN and FIBA.

Badri, B. and A. S. Badri 1990. Female Circumcision:Attitudes and Practices. In M Schuler,(ed.), *Women Law and Development in Africa.* White Plans, Maryland: Automated Graphic Systems.

Bernbaum, E. 2022. *Sacred Mountains of the World* (2 ed.). Cambridge: Cambridge University Press.

Bower, J. R. F. 1973. Early pottery and other finds from Kisii District, Western Kenya. *Azania,* VIII: 131–140.

Bronson, S., Jester, T. 1997. Conserving the built heritage of the modern era: recentdevelopments and ongoing challenges. *Assoc. Preserv. Technol. Bull.* 28 (4), 4-12.

Chaplin, J. H.1974. "The prehistoric rock art of the Lake Victoria Region". *Azania,* Vol. IX: 1–50.

Chaplin, J.H. and McFarlane, M.J. 1967. The Moniko Petroglyphs. *Uganda Journal,* XXXI, 207-8.

Eisemon, T.O. Hart, L.M. and Ongesa, E. 1988. *Stories in stone: Soapstone Sculptures from Northern Quebec and Kenya.* Quebec: The Canadian Museum of Civilization.

El-Dareer, A. 1978. Female Circumcision and the Current Preventive Efforts in the Sudan: Paper Presented at the XXI Meeting of the African Studies Association, Baltimore Maryland. Nov. 1-4, 1978.

Ermischer, G. 2004. Mental landscape: landscape as idea and concept. *Landscape Research,*29(4):371-383.

Fowler, P. 2004. *Landscapes for the World: Conserving a Global Heritage.* Macclesfield: Windgather Press.

Giorgis, W. B. 1981. *Female Circumcision in Africa.* Addis Ababa Research Series

Gluckman, M. 1962. *The Ritual of Social Relations.* Manchester: Manchester University Press

Gopal, Madan and K.S. Gautam (eds.). 1990. *India through the ages.* Publication Division, Ministry of Information and Broadcasting, Government of India.

Haring, Lee. 1974. Gusii Oral Texts. *The International Journal of African Historical Studies.* Vol. 7 (1): 107-119.

Hakansson, N. Thomas.1988. Bridewealth, Women and Land: Social Change among the Gusii of Kenya. *Uppsala Studies in Cultural Anthropology* 9. Stockholm: Almkvist and Wiksell International, .

Hakansson, N. Thomas. 1994. Detachable Women: Gender and Kinship in Processes of Socioeconomic Change among the Gusii of Kenya. *American Ethnologist* 21 : 516–538.

Hein, Carola, van Schaik, Henk, Six, Diederik, Mager, Tino, Kolen, Jan (J. C. A.), Ertsen, Maurits, Nijhuis, Steffen and Verschuure-Stuip, Gerdy.2020. Introduction: Connecting Water and Heritage for the Future. In Hein, C. (ed.), *Adaptive Strategies for Water Heritage,* https://doi.org/10.1007/978-3-030-00268-8 1. 1-16.

Huntington, J. 2003.*The circle of bliss Buddhist meditational art.* Serindia Publications.

ICOMOS Australia (International Council on Monuments and Sites Australia). 2000. *The Australian ICOMOS Charter for the Conservation of Places of Cultural Significance (The Burra Charter)*. Sydney: ICOMOS Australia.

Inyega, K. O. *Development of Cultural Tourism in Kisii*, in Akama, J. S., and Maxon, R. (ed), *Ethnography of the Gusii Western Kenya: A Vanishing Cultural Heritage.* The Edwin Mellen Press, U.S.A 2006. New York. (a copy is attached).

Ingold, T. 1993. The Temporality of the Landscape. *World Archaeology* 25(2):152-74.

Islamic Sheria Law 2015. *Punishment for adultery in Islam*. *Religious tolerance.org. Archived from the original on 9 January 2015. Retrieved 26 February 2022.*

Jopela, A. 2018. "Reorienting Heritage Management in Southern Africa: Lessons from Traditional Custodianship of Rock Art Sites in Central Mozambique." In W. Ndoro, S. Chirikure, and J. Deacon(eds), *Managing Heritage in Africa: Who Cares?* 55–71. London: Routledge.

Kenyatta, Jomo. 1961.*Facing Mount Kenya*. London: Secker and Warburg.

Kiangoi, J. 1977. Indigenous Gusii system of administration of justice with particular reference to the procedure followed in settlement of legal studies. LLB Dissertation, University of Nairobi.

Kiriama, H. O.1986. My roots and their importance in understanding Abagusii history. *Transafrican Journal of History*, 15: 191-201.

Kiriama, H. O. 1987. Archaeo-metallurgy of iron smelting slags from a Mwitu Tradition site in Kenya. *South African Archaeological Bulletin*, 42: 125 – 130.

Kiriama, H. O. 2021. Heritage Management in East Africa. In Shadreck Chirikure (ed), *Oxford Research Encyclopedia of Anthropology.* New York: Oxford University Press.

Kiriama, H.O. 2017. Memory, Identity and Heritage in the south Kenya Coast: Case of Shimoni Slave caves. *Journal of African Cultural Heritage Studies* 1:4-18.

Kiriama, H. O and Onkoba, E. N. 2020. Significance in African Heritage. In Daniela Turcanu-Carutiu (ed), *Heritage.* London, InTechOpen. 175-210.

Kohn, E. 2013. *How Forests Think: Toward an Anthropology Beyond the Human.* Berkeley, University of California Press.

Komma T. 1992. *Language as an Ultra – Human Power and the Authority of Leaders as Marginal Men: Rethinking Kipsigis Adminstrative Chiefs in the Colonial Period.* Senri Ethnological, Studies, Kanagawa University, Japan.

Langat, C. 1969. *Some Aspects of Kipsigis History Before 1914.* East African Publishing House, Nairobi.

Leakey, M.D.N. 1948. *Dimple-Based Pottery from Central Kavirondo, Kenya Colony.* Nairobi, Coryndon Memorial Museum.

LeVine, Robert A., et al. 1994. *Child Care and Culture: Lessons from Africa.* Cambridge: Cambridge University Press, .

LeVine, Robert A. and Barbara B. LeVine. 1966. *Nyansongo: A Gusii Community in Kenya.* Six Cultures Series, Vol. II. New York: John Wiley and Sons.

LeVine, Sarah. 1979. *Mothers and Wives: Gusii Women of East Africa.* Chicago: University of Chicago Press.

Mabbett, I.W. 1983.The Symbolism of Mount Meru. *History of Religions* 23 (1): 64–83

MacEachern, S. 2001. Cultural Resource Management and Africanist Archaeology. *Antiquity,* 75: 866–71.

Mason, R. 2002 Assessing Values in Conservation Planning: Methodological Issues and Choices. In Marta de la Torre (ed), *Assessing the Values of Cultural Heritage: Research Report.* Los Angeles The Getty Conservation Institute,

Maxon, R.M.1976. Gusii Oral Texts and the Gusii Experience under British Rule. *The International Journal of African Historical Studies,* 9 (1):74-80.

Maxon, R. M. 1972. Gusii resistance to British rule and its suppression, 1908. *Transafrican Journal of History,* 2,(1): 64-82.

Mbiti, J. S. 1975. *Introduction to African Religions, Second Revised Edition,* Nairobi: East Africa Education Publishers Ltd.

Messerli, B., and Jack D. Ives 1997.*Mountains of the World: A Global Priority.* 17. International Mountain Society, 39–54.

Mokua Z. O., Kiriama, H. O., Nyamwaka, E. O. and Oino, P. G. 2022. Promotion of Morality of Traditional Marriage among Abagusii through a Curse (Amasangia). *The East African Journal of Historical and Social Sciences Research*, 5(1), pp. 43–50.

Mokaya, D. M. 2012. *Female Circumcision Among the Abagusii of Kenya*. Nsemia Incorporated Publishers.

Moronya H. 2013. *Amasangia Egati Y'omogusii Korwa Ntuka*. Unpublished document.

Muthee, C. 1996. The Logic Behind Circumcision. *The People*, No. 178, Nairobi, Kalamka Ltd., July 19-25.

Naess, A. 1995. *Mountains and Mythology*. Trumpeter.

Ndeda, M. A.J. 2019. Population movement, settlement and the construction of society to the east of Lake Victoria in precolonial times: the western Kenyan case", *Les Cahiers d'Afrique de l'Est / The East African Review*, 52, 83-108.

The Bible, New International Version. Matthew 14:23. Jesus Prays at the Mountain.

Ng'ang'a, W. 2006. *Kenya's Ethnic Communities*. Nairobi, Gutundu Publishers Limited.

Northcote, G. A. S. The Kisii, KNA: DC/KSI/3/2

Ochieng, W. R. 1974. *A Pre-colonial History of the Gusii of Western Kenya from CAD 1500 to 1914*. East African Literature Bureau.

Ochieng, W. R. and Maxon, R. M. 1992. *An Economic History of Kenya. Transafrican Journal of History*. Vol 22:209-213.

Odak, Osaga 1977. Kakapeli and Other Recently Discovered Rock Paintings in the Western Highlands of Kenya, Azania: Archaeological Research in Africa, 12(1): 187-192, DOI: 10.1080/00672707709511254.

Odede, F. Z.A, Hayombe, P., Agong, S. G. A. 2014. Rock Paintings and Engravings in Suba Region along the Eastern Shores of Lake Victoria Basin, Kenya. *International Journal of Business and Social Research*, Vol. (10):15-24.

O'Neil, Dennis. "Culture and Society." Human Culture: What Is Culture?, 6 May 2006.

Ongesa, E. 2011. *Kisii Stone Sculpture.* Makerere University, School of Fine Art.

Onyambu, M. and Akama, J. 2018. The Evolution and Resilience of the Gusii Soapstone Industry, Journal of African Cultural Heritage Studies, 1 (1), 1 – 17.

Orchardson, I. 1971. *The Kipsigis.* EALB. Nairobi.

Partington, H. B. 1905. "Some Notes on the Kisii People," *East African Quarterly,* II, 4.

Pearson, M., & Sullivan, S. 1999. *Looking After Heritage Places, The Basics of Heritage Planning for Mangers, Landowners and Administrators.* Melbourne University Press.

Raivo, P. and Antonnen, M. 2004. *Historical Landscape and Geographical Memory.* Finnish Historical Landscape Project.

Ramsar 1994. Convention on wetlands of international importance especially as waterfowl habitat, with the amendments of 28.5.1987 and certified copy of 13.7.1994 by UNESCO. UNESCO, Paris

Resnick, M. 1998. *Kirinyaga: a fable of Utopia.* Ballantine.

Rockel S. 2006. *Carriers of culture: labor on the road in nineteenth-century East Africa.* Oxford: James Currey

Rutto B. 2016. *Kipsigis Heritage and Origin of Claw.* Nairobi, Ramco Printing Works Ltd, Kenya.

Sharfman J 2017. *Troubled waters. Developing a new approach to maritime and underwater cultural heritage management in Sub-Saharan Africa,* vol 41. Archaeological Studies, Leiden University, Leiden

Shepherd, G. 2004.*The Ecosystem Approach: Five Steps to Implementation.* IUCN, Gland, Switzerland and Cambridge, UK.

Snarman, M. 1971. *Man, Civilization and Conquest: From Pre-history to World Exploration.* London: Evans Brothers Ltd.

Silberschmidt, Margrethe. 1999.*"Women Forget that Men are the Masters": Gender Antagonism and Socio-Economic Change in Kisii District, Kenya.* Stockholm: Elanders Gotab.

Sinamai, A. 2019. *Memory and cultural landscape at Khami World Heritage site Zimbabwe: an uninherited past.* London, New York

Sinamai, A. 2021. Ivhu Rinotsamwa: Landscape Memory and Cultural Landscapes in Zimbabwe and Tropical Africa. *eTropic* 21.1 (2021) :51-69

Somjee, S. 2000. Oral Traditions and Material Culture: An East Africa Experience. *Research in African Literatures* **31**(4):97–103. doi:10.2979/RAL.2000.31.4.97. S2CID 144020233.

Taylor, K. and Lennon, J. L . 2011. Cultural landscapes: A bridge between culture and nature? *International Journal of Heritage Studies,* 17(6):537-554. http://flinders.edu.au – Understanding cultural landscapes: definition

Van Gennep A, 1972. *Rites of Passage.* Chicago: University of Chicago Press.

van Schaika, Henk; van der Valkb, Michael and Willems, Willem. 2015. Water and Heritage: conventions and connections. In Willem J.H. Willems & Henk P.J. van Schaik (eds). *Water and heritage: material, conceptual and spiritual connections:* 19-35. Leiden, Sidestone Press.

Verschuuren, B. 2006. An Overview of Cultural and Spiritual Values in Ecosystem Management and Conservation Strategies. Paper contributed to the International Conference on Endogenous Development and Biocultural Diversity, October 2006, Geneva, Switzerland (Available at: http://topshare.wur.nl/naturevaluation/75146).

Westerdahl Chr 1992. The Maritime Cultural Landscape. *Int J Naut Archaeol* 21(1):5–14

Zimmermann, Kim Ann. "What Is Culture? | Definition of Culture." LiveScience, Purch, 12 July 2017, Available here.

About the Authors

Prof. John S. Akama holds a PhD in Geography from Southern Illinois University, USA. For over 15 years, he taught at Moi University in Kenya, where he rose from the position of lecturer to the rank of Professor. While at Moi University, he taught students at both undergraduate and postgraduate levels. Over the years, Prof. Akama has conducted research and published widely in areas of culture, sociology, tourism, and wildlife management. His published works include *The Gusii of Kenya: Social, Economic, Cultural, Political & Judicial Perspectives,* (Nsemia Inc., 2017) and *The Untold Story: Gusii Survival Techniques and Resistance to the British Colonial Rule* (Nsemia Inc., 2019). He has co-authored many others including *Gusii Soapstone Industry: Critical Issues, Opportunities, Challenges & Future Alternatives* (Nsemia Inc., 2018) with Mallion Onyambu; *Enchengeria - EkeGusii Dictionary: The Complete EkeGusii Trilingual Dictionary* (Nsemia Inc., 2023) with co-editors Peter Nyansera Otieno, Peter Nyamache Getenga and Evans Gesura Mecha; and *Ethnography of the Gusii of Western Kenya* (Mellen Press, 2016) co-edited with Robert Maxon.

Prof. Akama was the founding Vice Chancellor of Kisii University, Kenya, where he was first appointed as founding Principal when the institution was a Constituent College of Egerton University before being made Vice-Chancellor when the institution acquired its Charter in 2013 to become a full-fledged University. The publication *Undeterred: A Rural Boy's Journey to the Pinnacle of Academia* (Nsemia Inc., 2021), written with Joshua Araka, is Prof. Akama's autobiography.

Prof. Herman Kiriama trained in Archaeology and Heritage Management at the University of Cambridge, UK and Deakin University, Australia, respectively. He has held several academic and professional posts, including being Head of Coastal Archaeology at the National Museums of Kenya, Programme Officer at ICCROM in Rome, Italy, Coordinator of Immovable Heritage at the Centre for Heritage Development in Africa, Head of Projects at the Australian Cultural Heritage Management in Melbourne, Australia and Visiting Professor, Peking University, Beijing, China and Coordinator of Research and Extension at Kisii University among many other responsibilities. Currently, Herman is an Associate Professor of Heritage Studies at Kisii University, Kenya and an Adjunct Associate Professor of Archaeology at La Trobe, University, Australia. He is also a Principal Consulting Archaeologist at Tardis Archaeology, Melbourne, Australia. He has written extensively on archaeology, heritage issues, memory and identity. He is the author of *The Legacy of Slavery in Coastal Kenya: Memory, Identity and Heritage (2022)* and co-author of *Slave Heritage and Identity on the Kenya Coast (2014).* Herman is also is co-editor of the widely used book- *Environmental Impact Assessment in Africa; A Review. Sacred Natural Sites and Cultural Heritage in East Africa (2010).* He is also the founding co-editor of *The African Journal of Heritage Studies* as well as editor of the *East African Journal of Historical and Social Sciences Research*

Joshua N. Araka is a multi-talented and award-winning photojournalist, creative writer, satirist, editor, biographer and researcher. He has so far authored four books: *Peppered Path*; *Chronicles of the Idler* (Nsemia Inc., 2022),; KorondoPanic and *The Surgeon Who Married Maria and Other Stories*. His prowess in biographies is evident in *Undeterred: A Rural Boy's Journey to the Pinnacle of Academia* (Nsemia Inc., 2021), co-authored with Prof. John S. Akama, and *Beaten Odds: Footprints of Uncertainty, Resilience, Adventure and Triumph* (Nsemia Inc., 2020), co-authored with Stephen Mabea. He also does media consultancy.

www.ingramcontent.com/pod-product-compliance
Lightning Source LLC
Chambersburg PA
CBHW020956160726
47994CB00006B/2251